Also by Anna Quindlen
Available from Random House Large Print

**Alternate Side**

**Miller's Valley**

**Still Life with Bread Crumbs**

# Nanaville

# Nanaville

## Adventures in Grandparenting

# Anna Quindlen

RANDOM HOUSE
LARGE PRINT

Copyright © 2019 by Anna Quindlen

Published in the United States of America by Random House Large Print in association with Random House, an imprint of Penguin Random House LLC, New York.

Cover design: Anna Bauer Carr
Cover photograph: DenisNata/Shutterstock

The Library of Congress has established a Cataloging-in-Publication record for this title.

ISBN: 978-0-5931-5301-7

www.penguinrandomhouse.com/large-print-format-books

FIRST LARGE PRINT EDITION

Printed in the United States of America

10  9  8  7  6  5  4  3  2  1

This Large Print edition published in accord with the standards of the N.A.V.H.

For
Arthur Krovatin

—————

**Wo ai ni, sunzi**

# Nanaville

Sunlight spreads across the checkerboard tiles in the kitchen, and so do many other things: wooden spoons, a rubber frog, Tupperware, a couple of puzzle pieces, some plastic letters, elements of the obstacle course of the active toddler. Did you know that the wheels on the bus go round and round, all through the town? They do, over and over again, sung by the robotic voice of some plastic magnetic thing on the refrigerator. Oh, and Old MacDonald has a farm. The hokey pokey? That's what it's all about.

This soundtrack, I know, will continue into perpetuity, first the nursery song, then the pop song, the rock song, the earworms of motherhood that emanate from the toy radio, the computer, from behind a closed bedroom door with a placard that says PLEASE KNOCK. I have been here before. Sort of.

A little hand rests lightly on my leg, a pale starfish of almost no weight, so that I might not know it was there were I not looking down at it as though it were the Mona Lisa, the Pyramids, the Sistine Chapel ceiling. Look at those fingers! Those tiny pillowy knuckles! When Shakespeare wrote, "What a piece of work is man," he must have been looking at a baby, I think to myself, which makes pretty clear that some crazy switch has been flipped in my brain. The wheels on the bus go round and round.

"Nana," he says softly, in a high voice that I know from experience will someday be deep and sonorous. But not now. Now it is sweet and light, like something produced by one of the small woodwinds.

"Yes, sweetheart," I reply.

"Nana," he says again.

"I'm here."

"Nana!" This time demanding, slightly petulant. And that's when I notice that he is looking at the fruit bowl on the table and when I realize that he is not crooning my name at all, my new name, of which I am so proud.

He just wants a banana and the full word is too much for him at this moment in his development. "Nana" denotes a piece of fruit, not this woman who follows him around as though he were a drum major and she a marching band.

These are useful moments, when we are made to understand where we really rate in the topography of family, if we are smart enough to pay attention and humble enough to accept the verdict. I know you don't want to consider this if you're in the same position I am, and I keep hearing that there are people who pay the notion no mind, but we grandparents are secondary characters, supporting actors. We are not the leads. Mama. Daddy. These are the bedrock.

We know this from past experience, our own experience. We were mother and father, most of us, before we became grandmother and grandfather. And because of that it is sometimes hard to accept that we have been pushed slightly to the perimeter. We are now the people whose names come in the smaller print in the movie credits. It's not that we are unimportant, as anyone who has ever had a grandparent knows. After all, secondary characters are what flesh out the plot: what would **Great Expectations** be without Miss Havisham, or **Romeo and Juliet** without the nurse? Mrs. Hudson may not get as much time in the stories as Sherlock Holmes does, but a reader is always very happy to have her show up.

The central figures of my childhood were my mother and father, but an essential part of the plot was my pink-skinned grandmother and gruff and demanding grandfather (Quindlen) and my dark and somber grandmother and gentlemanly grandfather (Pantano). They illuminated the story of where I had come from. Arthur's grandfather and I, my daughter-in-law's parents: it will be the same. We provide color, texture, history, mythology. But we are not central.

Mama means Mama. Daddy means Daddy.

But Nana might just be a piece of fruit.

Later on he will be able to say "apple" and "tractor" and even, rumor has it, "pterodactyl," although at the moment the last is such a welter of undifferentiated consonants that it would take a linguist, or a parent, to figure that out. Soon he has mastered the word "banana," and when he does, Nana becomes notably me. "Nana, please," he says when he wants something, often something he is not permitted to have. He is always happy to see me. He is not leveled by the leaving. On the evenings when I give him his dinner, his bath, and his bedtime stories, he sometimes cries as I put him in the crib because he realizes this means I'm all he has. "Mama and Daddy will be home soon," I say, the magic words.

His grandfather is Pop. For a while there was one word: "Nanapop." Sometimes there were three: "Nanapopgus." Gus is a Labrador retriever. That certainly puts things in perspective, doesn't it?

It's a complicated relationship, being a good grandparent, because it hinges on a series of other relationships. It's an odd combination of being very experienced and totally green: I know how to raise a child, but I need to learn how to help my child raise his own. Where I once commanded, now I need to ask permission. Where I once led, I have to learn to follow.

For years I had strong opinions for a living. Now I need to wait until I am asked for them, and modulate them most of the time. Probably I overreact. One day I wrote his parents an email about a school: "You should consider this for Arthur." I stared at the sentence and then changed it: "You might want to consider this for Arthur." Better to suggest than to command.

Because the kind of grandparent you are is partly determined by the relationship your child has with you, partly determined by the one a son or daughter has with his or her spouse, partly determined by the relationship you have with the person your child has chosen to have a child with.

It is determined by history, too, sometimes by what passed between you and your son and daughter many years ago, the things that have left an afterglow, or a scar. It is often determined by a relationship that most grandparents think they have mastered or at least successfully deconstructed: that is, being a parent. Ah, how we have convinced ourselves that there is no unfinished business, when adding another generation to the great human chain often excavates not so much the future as the past. It is interesting to discover how many people are disconcerted not because their parents are bad grandparents but because they are better grandparents than they were mothers and fathers. Or, as one woman said to me of her father, "He never took **me** to the movies," which might have seemed shabby and small to me had I not once bristled at the news that while my father never once turned the boat around when I was seasick, he was more than willing to do so for his grandchildren.

Most of us entered the parental enterprise with one of two impulses: to be as much like our own mother or father as possible, or to be unlike them in every conceivable way. And then we have children and discover what a difficult, circuitous, and ad hoc road our own parents traveled, and often our mindset changes. Or at least our behavior does. How many women have I known who vowed to be nothing like their own mothers and who found themselves slipping into old patterns in the press of the everyday? Conversely, I wanted to be as much like my mother as possible, which was often preposterous because I had a job other than child-rearing and she did not.

Eventually you discover that, at some level, you're just trying to get through the day without a trip to the emergency room. For me it was all a little like writing a novel. If I focused on the fact that I was producing an entire book, I was sunk. If I thought of it as a couple of good paragraphs a day, I managed to soldier through. If I focused on the fact that I was building a human from scratch, my head would explode. If I did one breakfast, one bath, one book, one bedtime, I was okay. I was supposed to have a philosophy, an ethos, abetted by endless thought and patience. Instead, I had **Sesame Street** and occasional McNuggets. In the words of the lyrics in the musical **Dear Evan Hansen** about mothering, "I'm flying blind, and I'm making this up as I go."

But being a grandmother isn't like that. You're not making the cake, or even the frosting; you're basically in charge of those little sugar flowers at the corners. And the role has changed so much since my own grandmothers were filling it. Being a grandparent is actually a fairly modern invention; for millennia, humans simply didn't manage to grow old enough to make it that far along the generational continuum. The big breakthrough was in the last century or so, when older people began to live longer and children to survive their childhoods. The research showing that people didn't become grandparents until fairly recently in human history also describes the value of the relationship: that sense of continuity, extended family, stories and legends passed down through the decades.

One of the quotes everyone seems to like about the relationship between grandparents and grandchildren is that they share a common enemy; I don't like that one, and I don't find it apt. We have a common nexus. There's no moment more eye-opening for a little kid than when you need to explain that Pop is Daddy's daddy. It's mind-boggling, the idea that Daddy was ever a little boy, that he was ever anything other than the towering colossus that casts a long shadow over life, that there was a time when Mama was a little girl instead of the source of all things.

Being Nana isn't, as some people have suggested, my reward for the thankless job of raising my own children. I really liked raising my own children, and my reward for that is them. I'm not delighted to be able to allow my grandson to do things at my house that he's forbidden at his own; it was kind of cute, the way my father loved to ply my three with Cocoa Puffs and Yodels, knowing there wasn't a snowball's chance of eating those things at my house, but I'm not inclined to follow his lead. That way is dangerous. In the way siblings fill the job not already taken—"Oh, you're the responsible, reliable one? Yippee! I'm going to have me some fun!"—so do grandparents have a natural tendency to segue into a role not occupied by a child's mother and father. But since it is in the very nature of good parenting to be responsible and reliable, what that can sometimes mean as a grandmother is positioning yourself as the fun one. Which may be fun for you, and fun for the grand-kids, but not so much fun for Mom and Dad. Hence the persistent grandparent mythology that the job is inherently to indulge and spoil, which casts Nana not as the bad cop and not even as the good cop but as the getaway driver.

One of the other tropes of the role is that there's a bit of a conspiracy between grandparent and grandchild. I think this is ill-advised. There are not that many things I'm sure of, but I'm certain that if you say to a six-year-old, for instance, "Don't tell Daddy we stayed up until eleven watching that movie I loved when I was a kid," before you can say, "We're back!" that child will start a sentence, "Nana told me not to tell you that . . ." This is not conducive to an atmosphere of trust. And trust is essential, not just to your relationship with your grandchildren but with their parents.

A good deal of being a grandparent is making it up as you go, particularly because of your peripheral place in the family dynamic. Care must be taken, boundaries respected. For the sake of amity I'm more invested in fitting into our grandson's routine than in busting him out of it, in having him be not a wedge issue but yet another bridge between his parents and me. I don't want to tell my son and his wife what to do; I'm not sure I know. I look at my kids and I have some vague sense of what paid off, what worked and what didn't, and what mistakes I didn't make. But it's very vague indeed. Many years ago someone handed me a brace of humans and said, essentially, Do your best. And I did some of the time, and some of the time, truth be told, I did my average, and occasionally I was kind of a bust. But if you sat me down and asked me why they turned into responsible and likable adults, I'm not sure I could answer in any coherent way.

I do know that a whole lot of love, in the words of Led Zeppelin, is always a good thing, and between the aunt, the uncle, the grandparents, and all the friends, there's no question that Arthur will have that.

Certainly he has a nana who has whole-heartedly embraced the role. I have become a woman who prepares to put on jewelry and then thinks to herself, no, those are bad nana earrings, a clear invitation to a tug. There are all these T-shirts for sale, with nana slogans: MY FAVORITE PEOPLE CALL ME GRANNY; PROMOTED TO GRANDMA; SPOIL THEM AND SEND THEM HOME. But who needs a T-shirt? Everyone can see you coming a mile away, the woman with the salt-and-pepper hair pushing a stroller. Waitresses totally have your number: Oh, he's so cute. Look at how well he ate his lunch (all the potato chips, a corner of the sandwich). So so adorable. What a big boy. Just flip a large bill on the table and call it a day. Did you ever think you would once again be saying to the hostess, "We need a high chair"?

I've never worried about feeling old because I'm a grandmother. I just feel blessed, which is apparently a common reaction, since a lot of those T-shirts on offer say BLESSED NANNY. I love this new stage because it gives me a second chance, to see, to be, to

understand the world, to look at it and rei-
magine my place in it, to feel as though I've
made a mark. They call them descendants,
but I don't care for that term. Descend?
No. They're elevators, really, rising above the
blind spots of my generation and even those
of their parents, going onward and upward.

"It's the best," my best friend said when
it happened to her.

"The best," said a woman across the table
at a dinner party.

"The best," said a stranger in line at
Target.

At a certain point you realize there's a
higher level of agreement about grandchildren than there is about the benefits
of democracy, or chocolate. Over and over
again, when people learned that our son and
his wife were expecting, or had a newborn,
or that they were bringing the baby over: it's
the best. Everyone talks about how great it
is, but I'm not sure it's possible to really feel
that until it's actually happened to you, until
you're really in it, which is probably a tiny
bit of useful protection for those people for
whom it will never happen, for one reason

or another. And it's a little challenging to suss out why exactly it can be so magical, since at some level it's about the oversight of children, which grandparents have experienced because they've already had children or they wouldn't have grandchildren.

All I know is: The hand. The little hand that takes yours, small and soft as feathers. I'm happy our grandson does not yet have sophisticated language or a working knowledge of personal finance, because if he took my hand and said, "Nana, can you sign your 401(k) over to me?" I can imagine myself thinking, well, I don't really need a retirement fund, do I? And, besides, look at those eyelashes. Or the greeting. Sometimes Arthur sees me and yells "Nana!" in the way some people might say "ice cream!" and others say "shoe sale!" No one else has sounded that happy to see me in many many years.

I remember sitting on the porch in a rocker and watching Arthur toddle across the lawn, his fat thighs parenthetical, his arms raised in that triumphant gesture that looks like a celebration but is clearly meant mainly to steady a still-unsteady walker. It was as though all the dust motes dancing in the summer sunshine coalesced around him, so that he had a nimbus of light, like the Christ Child in a Renaissance painting. And, by the way, that simile is purely intentional.

Why the depth of feeling? Babies do tend to bring that out in most of us, even when they are not related to us directly. There's the theory that we respond viscerally to entities with big heads, big bellies, and big eyes—which also explains why audiences were enamored of E.T.—that there is something within us that cries out to preserve and protect them.

But in terms of this specific baby, I often think of a poem I encountered for the first time when I was babysitting for a couple whose children were adopted:

**Not flesh of my flesh,**
**Nor bone of my bone,**
**Yet somehow miraculously my own.**
**Don't ever forget for a single minute**
**You didn't grow under my heart, but**
**   in it.**

It's different with a grandchild. He hasn't grown under your heart, but he's part of your flesh, only secondhand. Your baby's baby. It seems absurd when the baby is bearded, bass-voiced, big-footed, smarter than you are. And yet there's something about having this little boy that makes you look at the big picture, turn the telescope around so that you're suddenly aware of the continuum, not only of your own life but of where you've come from and where you're going.

And, above all, becoming a grandparent offers a chance to love in a different way, a love without the thorny crown of self-interest. I wish I could say I loved my children that way, but it wouldn't be true, and it wouldn't be true of anyone I know, either. There is always that part of you, that shame-making part, that sees everything from toilet training to college honors as a reflection on how well you've done your job. The mother who sits in the darkened auditorium mouthing the actor's lines because she has been running lines with the actor for weeks is not a disinterested party. The curtain call is, in part, her triumph.

I can tell you that unequivocally because I was that mother. Still am. Some years ago a man who has worked with their father witnessed our three grown children together at a hockey game, laughing and talking and getting along, as they now tend to do. That man wrote the loveliest letter about how terrific it was to witness this. That letter is in the box on my desk where I keep special keepsakes. It might as well have at the top, in red marker: "A+. Good work."

The great thing for me about being a grandmother is that no one is grading me in that way. My grandson doesn't reflect on my performance except that his existence is, in some manner, a reflection of my own. It's pretty immaterial to me at what age he learns to read, whether he has a good throwing arm or an eye for color and form. I am much more capable of seeing him purely as himself than I ever was with his father, his uncle, or his aunt.

I'm tempted, writing that, to think reflexively that that is a healthier way to be, to care, to love. But that's exactly the response I've learned not to have to being Nana. No best way. No right answer. What gives me pleasure is that this boy is surrounded by so many different iterations of love, and when I think back on my own family, I realize that was the buoy. It's like a meal, isn't it? Your parents are the protein, the chicken and the fish or maybe the tofu. Your aunts and uncles are around the edges, vegetables, salad. We grandparents, if we play it right, are dessert. Not the main course, surely, but something very sweet, which most people really like and want a piece of.

One day, when this boy was an infant and was being tetchy, I took him from his exhausted parents and muttered into the flower cup of his little ear, "You're going to the Nanaville Correctional Institution." Inmate no. 000000001, I called him, and I was the warden. He was incarcerated more than once during his infancy. It was mostly wonderful, for me if not always for him.

Nanaville has morphed now, from a tiny prison to a small town. Every once in a while we go there, my grandson and I. Population two, I say, although someday soon it will be three, and then maybe four or more.

My grandchildren will likely come to think of Nanaville as an actual place, the place where they sometimes stay. They will probably still come to sometimes think of it as being taken into custody, as well, being remanded to Nana for a meal, a movie, a trip, a day, or occasionally a week when their parents are willing, or busy, or maybe just want to have a life for a while.

But I think of Nanaville as a state of mind, a place I wound up inhabiting without ever knowing it was what I wanted, needed, or was working toward. People ask me sometimes how I came by my profession, and one answer lies in a moment when my eighth-grade teacher, Mother Mary Ephrem, looked up from her desk and said to me, "You are a writer." A declarative statement carries a powerful, almost undeniable sense of conviction.

"You are a grandmother," my son said one day in April, and I became something different than I'd ever been before. But becoming a nana is something different even than that, because it is being a grandmother in my own way, figuring out my rightful place in this new territory, with these new people. I am the mayor of Nanaville, and I vow to carry out my duties well.

# THIS IS HOW IT BEGINS

This is how it always begins: with an exclamation, a phone call, perhaps even the sound from the next room of a thready querulous cry, an inaugural announcement. World, I am born.

Or a text message.

**LYNN'S WATER BROKE. AT HOSPITAL NOW. STILL VERY EARLY IN PROCESS.**

I am in a hotel room in Baltimore, the morning after speechifying at a girls' school a few miles away. At 6:00 A.M. I wake to walk, run, or combine the two, depending on what my knees have to say about it, but before I do, I look at my phone, and there is the text from my eldest child, my elder son. He is about to become a father. I am about to become a grandmother. An estimated 360,000 people will enter the planet on this day, and my grandson is just one of them. Still, I feel as though the world has tilted on its axis.

I happen to have a very low resting heart rate and very low blood pressure. I think I feel both of them go sky-high. Knees or no, I run up to the girls' school campus where I spoke the night before, and back again. I want to get on an early train. I want to jump in a hired car. I want to go to the hospital. I want to rush into the delivery room. Instead, I take the Acela home, exactly as planned, and then sit at the dining room table with my second child, my younger son, who is about to become an uncle. He even has T-shirts at the ready: I'M THE CRAZY UNCLE EVERYONE WARNED YOU ABOUT, one says, and another says UNCLESAURUS. He is so ready. I am so ready. And yet, when the occasion arrives, not. We sit across from one another with the dumbstruck look of people trapped in the amber of a great moment with nothing to do, like actors backstage in the dark of the wings, waiting to go on. Several hours in, both of our phones buzz, and as though our movements are choreographed we each snatch them up and read.

BORN VIA EMERGENCY
C SECTION. TERRIFYING
EXPERIENCE. BUT HE AND
LYNN MADE IT. 7 LBS 9
OUNCES. WILL UPDATE AGAIN
ONCE I'M WITH LYNN IN
RECOVERY.

This is how it begins. Or maybe this is not the beginning at all. You could say it began when a young man walked into a bar in Beijing and met a young woman or, for the more conventional, the moment when those two people traded vows in the chambers of a judge and then in a field in Pennsylvania. Or when that same young man was born in New York City and the young woman in Beijing. Or, further back still, to his people coming to America from across Europe, to her Han Chinese family. Every baby arrives trailing endless ribbons of DNA, a microcosm of history, nationality, ethnicity, family. Somewhere in this infant is a trace of my mother, my father, the parents of Arthur's grandfather, the grandparents of my daughter-in-law, people he will never meet or know but who are embedded within him. I remember reading about the discovery of the remains of Richard II of England beneath a parking lot and the confirmation of their authenticity—more than five hundred years after the king's death—by the mouth swab taken from a Canadian-born cabinetmaker. Scientists figured out that some bones in the Russian countryside were those of the last tsar and his murdered family by analyzing genetic material from Prince Philip, who was not yet born when they were killed. People spit into a tube and a lab somewhere tells them whether they are Slavic or Scottish, Native American or Mexican. Each human is, in some way, a long long story, a saga with a beating heart, and our grandson is no different.

There's an entire history in every baby, even before that baby's own story has truly begun. As he figures out how to focus his eyes, as she manages to roll over, as he crawls and she walks and he talks and she runs, we intuitively feel ourselves watching the progression of existence. Better still, we appreciate it all over again. Look at the trees. Taste the applesauce. Kiss Mama. Hug Daddy. Take chances. Fall down and cry and stand and fall again. Feel safe. Each baby is the homunculus, that small human dreamed up by alchemists hundreds of years ago, not only the beginning of his own story but a plotline in a larger one, a branch on an enormous tree. A son. A nephew.

A grandbaby.

Of course, when we finally meet Arthur Krovatin for the first time, he is just a bundle in a blanket with a full head of glossy black hair. There is only the promise of things to come: steps, words, school, work, marriage, children of his own. The future. And when I first saw him in the hospital, the day after my elder son's terrifying experience, I did not really see him himself. This is always the problem, isn't it, our natural inability to see a child as himself alone, not hung about from the first with similarities, expectations, and assumptions like the familiar ornaments on a Christmas tree. I couldn't help noticing that Arthur had a good deal of hair, as his father, his mother, his aunt, and his grandmother had had as newborns; I couldn't help noticing that he looked beautifully Chinese, which was something my own grandfathers would have found astounding and, probably, disconcerting. Because of the speed with which his mother had wound up in surgery, our son had only managed to stand in the doorway while the actual incision and extraction was happening. Because of the speed with which the surgery had been necessary, an obstetrician who had never met my daughter-in-law before did the procedure and, looking at the baby's father, said quizzically, "This baby looks Asian."

"The mother is Chinese," a nurse said, and the doctor looked over the surgical drape and said, "Oh, hello."

"Thank you," said my daughter-in-law.

Standing in the hospital room, watching

her try to find a comfortable position after abdominal surgery, watching my son crumple their carefully crafted birth plan in his hand (natural birth, no epidural; so much for the best-laid plans), I felt for them. They will never forget this day, just as I will never forget the days on which I gave birth to my children. But it will pale next to the day-to-day of having a child. One of the most resonant moments of my past was when I had the first contraction the second time around. I was immediately overwhelmed with muscle memory and incredulity: why in the world did I decide to go through this again? The answer was simple. It was because the first time it had been such a trip, watching this big-eyed big-headed big-bellied person change by inches, until in what seemed like no time at all he went from a crumpled little vermilion face and terrifying cone head in a birthing room to this tall dark man holding his own newborn son.

I don't have precisely that time-lapse experience with our grandson now because, although we see him often, we don't see him every day. I miss some of the synapses, which means I am always rediscovering him. This gives your grandchildren a certain allure, a kind of mystery that your children seldom have. From time to time I will say, "I wonder what Arthur is doing." Since I was with them all the time, I rarely wondered what my own three were doing, unless there was a loud crash from upstairs. Occasionally when they were at college I would idly wonder what they were doing, but then my mind would take a sharp left turn into some safer cul-de-sac of contemplation, like whether there was yogurt for breakfast or the recycling was due to be picked up in the morning.

Mothers know the day-to-day; nanas wonder between times of togetherness. It's one difference, but there are many. I have no text message, no date or time to mark the moment I truly became Nana. I can't remember what day it was, only how it happened:

**I am changing his diaper, he is kicking and complaining, his exhausted father has gone to the kitchen for a glass of water, his exhausted mother is prone on the couch.**

He weighs little more than a large sack of flour and yet he has laid waste to the living room: swaddles on the chair, a nursing pillow on the sofa, a car seat, a stroller. No one cares about order, he is our order, we revolve around him. And as I try to get in the creases of his thighs with a wipe, I look at his, let's be honest, largely formless face and unfocused eyes and fall in love with him. Look at him and think, well, that's taken care of, I will do anything for you as long as we both shall live, world without end, amen.

I can't remember when exactly I had that moment with my own children. I suspect it was different: that final exhausted terrible satisfying push, and then the feeling of vast responsibility. At some point, in our big brass bed, a few days removed from the hospital, I looked down at our first, the father of this first grandchild, and I felt a frisson like falling. Who the hell thought it was a good idea to send us home with a semi-cooked human? I thought. My son says it's called the fourth trimester, a term that must be new, because God knows I read everything when

I was pregnant and postpartum and never heard it. But it's apt, that feeling that maybe this person could have used a few more hours in the oven, so to speak. You watch on the giraffe cam, and that spindly-legged baby has a couple of hours to struggle with competence, and then it's on its feet. Humans are the animals whose newborns take the longest to get it together. Maybe that explains the love; it's hard to imagine not cleaving to a being so conspicuously needy. And not being afraid that you're somehow going to break it, too. I am the eldest of five, and Pop is the eldest of six; clearly we are two people who might have been assumed to know what it takes to care for an infant. But, oh, the responsibility of your own is indescribable until it falls on you like a house.

I feel a sense of great responsibility with Arthur, too, but being an old hand has its rewards. When he was very little and not on an easy footing with sleep, he would go seriously sideways in the late afternoons. "He's inconsolable," his grandfather said, inconsolable himself. It was true. Existential angst stripped down to its essence. The air, the sunlight, the feeling of cotton on skin, the feeling of moving through space, the effort of holding a head on a neck, a neck on the shoulders: it all seems terrifying when you not only have never done it but when you're so absent any other thoughts or distractions that it is what fills your mind. But I knew that this would pass. I knew that a wailing infant is nothing compared to an unhappy teenager. Also that sometimes if you put babies belly down on top of the dryer while it's running they will soothe. When he was inconsolable, I wanted to take Arthur to the basement.

In other words, I wanted to take hold, to act, to do something.

But as a grandmother and not the mother, I have to temper that. That day awaiting news at the dining table, both Christopher and I wanted to do something, but we did not. My daughter-in-law had not asked me to join her in the birthing room, and I have to admit that I was a little disappointed, reading all those stories about women who stood at the foot of the bed while a grandchild emerged, lovely and yucky. Like most decisions my daughter-in-law has made since I have known her, this one was absolutely correct. I can imagine myself in the hospital that day. I have a bit of a sideline in practicing medicine without a license or, some people might argue, not much of a clue, and my inclination would have been to ask too many questions, make a fuss, all while someone else was actually having contractions. Not a good look, or a good benchmark for the future. "Begin as you mean to go on," a British preacher once said many many years ago, and, boy, is that good advice on delicate human relations.

But it can all go wrong for my generation of what have come to be called helicopter parents, who have not only overseen but have engineered and interfered in the lives of their children. Those impulses are powerful, even for those of us who like to believe we have not yielded to them.

(I qualify this assessment of my own mothering in the face of one afternoon when I gave a speech that, for some reason, all three of my children were attending. I mentioned in passing that I knocked off my writing day when they were young an hour before I went to pick them up at school, so that I could successfully morph from writer to single-minded mother. The look of incredulity on all three of their faces as I said this made manifest that the morphing had been unsuccessful.)

What's expected of new parents is rather clear, and clearly task-based, at least at first. But it's less clear for grandparents. The first time I saw Arthur, in that hospital room, I reached for him reflexively and then stopped. "Can I pick him up?" I asked my daughter-in-law, testing the waters. "Of course," she said, signaling right at the start where I stood. I cannot emphasize that more strongly for those of you in this situation. The matter-of-fact tone of voice, the sense that I was obviously entitled—our first grandchild's mother was sending a message of clear permission. It made all the difference. It will make all the difference. Whether grandparents of a toddler or teenager, we know we are part of the program.

This goes both ways, of course. I'd like to think that I sent a message that day, too, that I would be careful and thoughtful, neither one of which I'm necessarily suited for by nature. Thank God that Christopher and I were together that afternoon at the dining table, or else I might have run the ten blocks south to the hospital and insinuated myself where I was not needed or wanted. Lesson one of being a grandmother: do not do that. Perhaps we make the mistake, having been handed an inchoate package of undifferentiated humanity with an umbilical stub once upon a time ourselves, that this will be just like that. It's not. Arthur is not exactly my job but a good deal more than a hobby. I suppose now being his nana is my avocation.

Someone else nurses the baby. Someone else decides whether he will be rocked to sleep or allowed to cry it out, whether he will be permitted his thumb or switched to a pacifier, whether he will be circumcised and weaned and shod. Someone else will choose his name, and if you don't like it you'd damn well better arrange your face as though you do, and soon enough you will discover that since it's his name you like it just fine, you love it, even.

So much of being a mother is doing things: feeding diapering reading chasing chastising lullabying lifting loving. But an important part of being a grandmother is that thing that mothers often find most challenging: hanging back. As my children got older it was terribly difficult for me not to rush into the breach. They would come home with a tale of a contretemps on the playground, a reprimand in the library. I remember the day my daughter was talking about some piece of conspicuous unfairness, and when she saw my face she said, in her fiercest fashion, "Mom, don't . . . call . . . anyone."

I didn't. But I wanted to.

Maybe this is why so much of being a grandparent feels like auditioning. The role of Mama and Daddy is self-evident. Grandparents? Not so much. Who are you and why are you here sometimes but not all the time? Where do you fit into my day-to-day? It feels like those are the thoughts of the little person and perhaps that explains why some of us try so hard. Maybe that's why some grandparents buy the things that are verboten, allow the TV time the parents won't. I certainly don't remember doing so much mugging and rolling around with my own kids, but I didn't have to show them that I was somehow significant. One day I even did a headstand for Arthur. He looked unpersuaded. I convinced myself that maybe when he was older he would be impressed, but then I pictured some rangy teenager sitting in a diner and saying to his buds, "My nana did a headstand in the living room last night."

"Dude," they would say. "Ah, dude." And not in a good way.

Of course, some of the auditioning, if not most, takes place not with the child but with the parents. If they have childhood grievances, this is the perfect forum in which to play them out like a game of charades. I read not long ago about a woman who gave her mother a three-page single-spaced memo before letting her babysit. Her mother! Who had at least one child that we know of—the woman handing her the memo!

Swallow hard, Grandma, and smile. It's all about spending time with the grandchild. No matter what the cost.

The thing is, from the moment it begins you want to do something. "Let me help," you say. And sometimes, if you're lucky, the people who really get to make all the decisions will let you do so, push the stroller for an hour while they get the dishes done, do the dishes while they go for the walk. It's their call. The torch is passed to a new generation, as well as the bouncy seat, and the breast pump, and the baby wipes. And, for most of the time, the child.

## SMALL MOMENTS

It's 2:07 A.M. on the digital-clock face. Out on the street it sounds as though two people are arguing, although the specifics are muffled because the windows are closed. It's stuffy in here, but better stuffy than drafty where someone else's infant child is concerned. Window open. Window closed. Window open. Closed again. This baby will not catch cold on Nana's watch!

His mother is a floor below, getting a good night's sleep. She could use it. Her husband is traveling on business, her son still nurses every few hours, and the day before, as she bent to lift him, she torqued something in her back. It's an occupational hazard they never mention to new mothers, that you need to soften your knees when you pick the baby up or you will suddenly feel a fire at the small of your back, the nerve down one leg or the other screaming. The stitches, the nipples, the lower back: it's as though all your body is sacrificed to the greater good after you've had a baby. I have taken over for the night and headed upstairs to the guest bedroom, which now has a crib as well as a bed.

The greater good makes a faint mewling sound from the embrace of a kind of soft cradle on a little metal stand. Plug it in and it rocks back and forth and plays a variety of sounds. You can choose whale calls, lullabies. I'm using white noise. It helps me sleep, too, although I am once again in the land of mom sleep, remembered from years before, when a snort in the next room can take you from out-of-it to wide awake in an instant.

2:09, and he's up. Ah ah ah. I lift him from the cradle in the old familiar hold, one hand under the head, the other under the butt. He is still in that stage of his development when he seems as formless as the swaddle in which he is wrapped, like bag-o-human. A huge head on an unreliable stem of neck, fist as likely to poke him in the eye as to catch hold of anything it flails toward. This must be nature's design. He is so pathetic and helpless that we have no choice but to dance attendance on him, even with sciatica. Not to mention that a baby wailing is one of the most unnerving sounds imaginable. You read over and over again that when people do bad things to their small children, it's to stop them from crying.

I have a bottle of breast milk expressed by his mother earlier in the evening. I've angled him so he is mainly in the dark, but the streetlights faintly pick out the pulse in his jaw as he sucks. He is warm and somehow companionable; it feels as though we are the only two people awake in the big city. The burp, the rocking, and then I put him back down. He is not pleased. I pick him up and rock him for a few more minutes. Still unhappy, he starts to complain more loudly. I know his mother has developed mom sleep, too, and I do not want to wake her. I take him from the cradle and put him next to me in the bed. On his belly he splays like a frog, arms and legs bent into angles, head turned to the side, mouth ajar and slack like an old man sleeping.

And he is indeed sleeping.

I am doing everything wrong here. He is not supposed to do what is called co-sleeping—that is, be in the same bed as the adults. Like everything else now about being a mother, there is endless argument online about this, about its dangers, its advantages. Not for the first time, I am glad that my babies predate the Internet. I had Dr. Spock and Dr. Brazelton and my own best instincts, powered less by science than by a combination of exhaustion and convenience. Sometimes I joined in with the symphony of flat-out lies on the play-ground, but at least I didn't have to comb through a constant barrage of judgment about the plastic in bottles and the toxins in detergents at the end of every advice article online.

He is also not supposed to be sleeping on his stomach. I cycled through prevailing medical opinion on sleep positions as a young mother. I was supposed to put the first on his stomach so that if he spit up he wouldn't aspirate it into his lungs. (I love it when you hear things like this. The doctor is saying very calmly, "Aspirate into his lungs" and you're nodding and thinking, **Aspirate? Into his lungs?**) Number two was supposed to be on his side. Have you ever tried to get a baby to sleep on his side? The package is not designed that way. By the third there was some debate, side or back. It seemed someone, somewhere, had decided the lung-aspiration danger no longer applied. I settled the matter with my youngest by choosing the position in which she was most likely to settle down. I had three children under the age of five. Pragmatism was my middle name. If she'd wanted to sleep upside down like a bat, I would have put a bar on the ceiling above the crib. Whatever gets you through the night.

But I am with someone else's baby, even

if I like to think of him as somehow partly
mine, and I cannot have that attitude.
Because now the consensus is strong, not
to say draconian: back-sleeping to guard
against sudden infant death syndrome.
Well, hell, throw the D word around to
new parents and you can just about guar-
antee compliance.

This has even given rise to a new phenomenon, called tummy time, because all
these back-sleeping babies are getting flat
heads. So now a couple of times a day we
are supposed to put Arthur on his stomach
so he will learn to lift his head and shoulders, kind of like Pilates, except that unlike
Pilates the lift is quite easy but the touch-
down is pretty graceless: He's up, then he
flops. Up, flops. When he flops he sometimes settles in, making it quite clear: this
baby is most comfortable lying on his
stomach. But he is not permitted to sleep
there. It's been all I can do not to say to his
parents, "Leave him alone. He's comfortable as is."

The faint light from the city street
makes a stripe across his back. Definitely

breathing. I synchronize my breath to his as we struggle through the night in Nanaville.

I want to leave this baby on his stomach so he will sleep soundly. I'm certain he will be fine. But I can't take a chance. So I lie in bed awake and carefully watch him breathe for three hours. This is the closest I've come to pulling an all-nighter since college. At 5:11 he starts to stir, a ribbon of silver snail-trail drool shining in the faint gray daylight from the street. I give him a second bottle. This time, after a minute or two of grousing, he settles into the rocking cradle and falls asleep on his back. And so do I. I hope his mother, on the floor below, is sleeping soundly, as well.

Lessons learned:

- Sometimes what feels like a favor winds up being a blessing.

- Sleeplessness is more survivable in small doses.

- White noise is wonderful. I put it on now every time I am sleeping in a hotel room, and whenever I do, like Proust with his madeleine, I go back to that moment, Nana and Arthur, side by side. Then I fall asleep, happy.

# BEYOND WORDS

The first sentence we learned was "I love you."

Wo ai ni. Wo ai ni, sunzi. I love you, grandson.

I don't like doing things I don't think I'm good at, which sometimes makes me wonder how I ever learned to do anything at all. I have long thought that I was bad at foreign languages; perhaps, as a writer, I hold my native tongue close and refuse to accept other comers. Once I had satisfied the college language requirement, I added that to the list of things I would never have to do again, which is a list that is now blessedly long. No more standardized tests. For that matter, no more pap tests. I'm done with résumés and job interviews.

And yet here I was, learning a foreign language that, as one of my friends noted helpfully, is about as tough as they come. Our first grandchild is half Chinese. His parents originally hired a Mandarin-speaking sitter, an ayi who kept careful notes, as beautiful as scrimshaw, about Arthur's day, pictograms interspersed with military time for naps and the occasional Englishism: "pupu" was my favorite, since I could understand what it meant.

The first time I came to relieve the ayi I said, "Ni hao," at the door, exhausting my entire repertoire with a hello except for the moment when she left, when I said, "Xiexie." Thank you. From that moment on, when I tried out my baby Chinese—did he eat applesauce? Does he like yogurt?—the ayi would wrinkle her brow and say, "Shenme?" which means "what?" but translates as "I know you are trying to speak Mandarin but I can't understand a word you are saying."

Arthur's parents both speak Mandarin: our daughter-in-law as her birthright, our son by dint of long study, considerable determination, and several years of living and working in China. At the wedding his father-in-law, who is a professor of classical Chinese, made much of the fact that our son had asked for his daughter's hand with ancient language and rite. "How romantic," I said when Quin told me what he planned. "Honestly, it's more like a transfer of property," he'd replied.

His in-laws say his Chinese is very good. How would I know? All I know is that I find learning this language so difficult—shaping the muscles of my mouth to make sounds I'm quite sure I've never made before—that in this, as in so many things, I am in awe both of my eldest child and by what my love for my grandson will lead me to do.

"You are doing very well!" said the lovely young woman who came once a week to sit at the dining room table and teach Arthur's grandparents her native tongue. She made our efforts easier by being so nice and so obviously touched by our impulse. At our first lesson—"Dui. Bu dui. Hao. Bu

hao"—she asked why we wanted to learn
Chinese. She said that she had had many
students who were young Chinese Americans
whose parents felt their language skills were
so deficient that they would have difficulty
communicating with their native grandparents. But she had never had grandparents
who wanted to learn to communicate with
their grandson. She was kind enough to
build all of our lessons around our likely
interactions with Arthur: Do you want to
go to the park? Do you like milk? Thus did
we find ourselves one evening launch-
ing into a full-throated rendition of "If
you're happy and you know it, pai pai shou."
Clap clap.

We don't have to do this. Our grandson,
his parents, his other grandparents, almost
everyone around him: we all speak English.
If Yeye and Nainai spoke only English to
Arthur, he would grow up understanding
the two of us just fine. Ditto for the grandparents who are native Mandarin speakers,
Laolao and Laoye. We all four speak quite
sophisticated English, rich, polysyllabic on
occasion. Our son once told us, on the way

home from the airport when he was visiting from China, that one of the things he found most challenging was not having access to that complex vocabulary, what might be called Graduate Level Mandarin, although it was most gratifying when a cab driver in Beijing told us our son's command of slang was excellent.

But becoming a touchstone for those people who extend my line consists of many parts, and learning some Mandarin feels like one of them. The reason why is simple, and undeniable. At least one set of my grandchildren will be bilingual, and I can already hear my grandson say, in a quizzical voice, "Nana, why can't you speak Chinese?" And it's not that I am competitive about this, as I am in so many other things. It's that I want to be in his world as much as I can without crowding him, or his parents. It's the linguistic equivalent of getting down on the floor to play with him at his own level. Chinese will not be the only way to do this, certainly. Someday, if I live long enough, I will want to know what he's studying in college and discuss it with him.

I will want to make pot roast for a crowd of his friends and eggs Benedict for his significant other. I will want to buy him something silly that he really wants for his birthday, and I will want to buy him a pair of theater tickets if I've seen something I really like and suspect he might like it, too.

And when he looks at the old Labrador and says "hei gougou" instead of "black dog," I want to understand. I want him to think his grandparents took the trouble to be where he is.

Because I'm learning that being a grandmother is not about the things you have to do. It's about the things you want to do. The fact is that motherhood is mainly about requirements. Very, very little of it is optional if you're doing it with even a modicum of care. There's no sitting on the couch with a cup of coffee and the remote control, saying to yourself, I don't really have to feed that baby. I don't have to change his dirty diaper. I don't have to keep an eye on the toddler when she's around the cat or take her to the pediatrician when she's a hot little bundle of bright red pulling at her ear and sobbing.

Motherhood is mainly a roundelay of Thou shalt, shalt, shalt.

Nana, unless she has become de facto Mom for some sad reason, is pretty much purely about desire. I've fed the baby, changed the diaper, crawled around on the floor while he went straight for the electrical outlet or the dog's tail. But I've done that because I offered and my offer was accepted. Most grandparents are tethered but not tied, connected but not compelled, except by choice.

Inevitably I will fall down on the job. Already I am keenly aware of some of my nana shortcomings. I have kind of a dirty mouth. It wasn't always so. I don't believe I swore, or what would now be called swearing, until I was in college. They were different times, of course. I distinctly remember an evening on which a casserole dish cracked as my mother was moving it from oven to counter and she lost the veal parmigiana, splat, all over the kitchen floor. When she yelled, "Goddamn it!" I thought the earth might shudder to a halt in its customary revolution. Honestly, it's the most profane I ever heard her be.

I am much more profane than that. In my defense, after convent school and a women's college, I spent the most formative years of my life in a graduate-level institution for the use of bad language: a newspaper newsroom. It was also aces for the use of great language. I am a nana with a rich vocabulary. Thank you, editors and colleagues.

The rich vocabulary I will pass along. The profanity I will try to curb. I know very well that if I just stopped in the park, with the dog's leash tangled around my ankles while I held desperately on to the stroller, and marked the moment by saying "^^@?***#" or words to that effect, it's a cinch that some version of the same thing would eventually come out of my grandson's mouth.

And that would be bad.

But of course it's not just bad language. It's bad behavior, too. Part of becoming a grandparent is deciding that you must bring your A game. When I lose my temper and yell at the dogs, I see a look of surprise and distress on my grandson's face. It's almost as though, before he has grown the carapace of maturity, he knows instinctively what is not right. So I try not to do what is not right. Which leads to an inevitable and daunting conclusion: we have to be our very best selves around our grandchildren. For that to be true we sometimes have to be different people than we are when we are just slogging through the day. Being a good grandparent means being a good person.

So I will do this as best I can. As best I can: those are words I remember from my time as the mother of small children, and I think of them often today. They are forgiving words. When they hired the ayi, Arthur's parents had a plan that he would be fully bilingual. But then the ayi moved back to China to help with her own grandson, and the Mandarin preschool program cost the earth, and the wheels started to come off the bus of that part of the operation. (When I was raising our kids, the wheels came off so often that eventually the operation I was running was like one of those cars on cinder blocks parked next to a chop shop: No wheels, doors, wipers. Just a chassis. A chassis of motherhood.)

This also happened with our Mandarin

lessons. Our teacher moved back to China because of visa issues, and though we kept talking about finding another, life intervened. Pop got busy. Nana got busy. Arthur learned to say "Ferdinand" and "flower" in English. But then he went to Hong Kong to see Laolao and Laoye and spoke mainly Mandarin during the visit. One day we were sitting on the kitchen floor—it was during the period when we did a lot of sitting on the kitchen floor—and he said something to me in Chinese. And here's the thing: I managed to figure out what he was saying! He wanted milk. Niunai! It was in one of our earliest lessons, along with my pivotal identity: "I am grandmother—Wo shi nainai." And milk he was given. Niunai. Arthur had expanded my world, pushed me into a place I entered uncomfortable and never expected to inhabit. I wonder how many times that will happen with my grandchildren in the years ahead. Music, movies, books, clothing, technology. I will try to deal. Will they appreciate it? That's not the point.

My daughter was entering puberty around

the same time that I was in perimenopause, and let me tell you, that was a time! Estrogen up, estrogen down, a category-four mood storm coming in from the east and then circling the kitchen. You know what? It was helpful. Because of my own situation, I was constantly thinking of hormones as controlled dangerous substances, and that gave me a better understanding of how Maria was thinking and feeling.

Trying to learn Chinese, even at the most basic level, did the same thing for me in my dealings with Arthur. He, too, is learning language from the ground up. Every sentence is a struggle. Every sentence is a triumph. One evening before bed we were watching his statutory fifteen minutes of **The Lion King**, and I said, "There's Rafiki." Arthur replied solemnly, "Rafiki is a mandrill."

The following thoughts flashed through my mind:

- A monkey with a wildly colored face: Rafiki **is** a mandrill. I never noticed that before.
- My son and daughter-in-law are the

world's best parents, because one of
them must have noticed and told
Arthur that Rafiki was a mandrill.
- Call the newspapers: toddler genius
in apartment 2B.

The thing about language is that it is the
ultimate transactional process. And I don't
just say that as a person who makes a living
playing Jenga with words. If you watch
children acquire language, you can see them
not only speaking but arranging the known
world. We ask them questions we know they
know the answers to—What color is that
ball? Where do the frogs live?—so that they
can practice the arrangement. It's also pretty
thrilling to be part of the process, and for
a grandparent it's tantamount to learning a
new dialect. Arthur was quite chatty as a
toddler and discursive in a way that meant
you had to pay attention and, like with
Mandarin, be aware of tones. Sometimes a
long string of sentences unfurled that definitely included the words "cows," "horns,"
"little," and "Dada," but it would take an
expert in simultaneous translation, like his

parents, to report that he had seen cows at the farm, and the male cow was a bull and had horns, and he was the dada of the calves, who were the little cows. It was storytelling as a way of feeling in control of the environment, which is, often without noticing it, what we all do throughout our lives.

But listening to stories and parroting them back—"You saw cows? And there was a daddy cow and he had horns?"—is not only reinforcing the importance of language, it's also reinforcing the importance of the individual. After all, it's only the people who think you have something to say who listen closely, and, conversely, it's the people who think you are unimportant who conspicuously ignore your stories and communicate that you're wasting their time and that they can't understand you.

When you do this with a child, when you struggle to understand them as they learn what is, at least for a moment, a foreign language, you are not simply indulging this in the present but for the future. We are all of us, mostly, familiar with the spectacular truculence of adolescents:

How was your day?

Fine.

What did you do?

Nothing.

Who were you with?

No one.

At this point, if your conversational part-
ner (if she can be called that) is a girl of
a certain ilk, she will scream, "Leave me
alone!" and exit the room. Most boys will
merely disappear by inches. Or maybe I'm
just extrapolating, and stereotyping, from
my own experience.

My point is that kids who grow up
thinking grandparents listen, really listen,
might throw an adverb or perhaps a short
description into that interchange. They
might even go further than they will with
their parents, who, they intuit correctly,
have so much invested in their interactions.
At the very least, they may understand from
past behavior that even though Nana is
way old—because, face it, when you're fifteen, anyone over forty has passed into a
different time zone—she may be relatively
unshockable and amenable.

Talking with a small child is like talking to yourself—yourself before you forgot to notice things. What evaporates as we age, sadly, is authenticity, that sense of saying your lines for the very first time. When Arthur is running in front of the spray of the hose with his arms outstretched, there is nothing but sensation: the water, the sunshine, the feel of both on his skin. There is no subtext, just text. Just the moment. I suppose the greatest gift we can give to children we love is to make it possible for them to hold on to that for as long as possible.

But it is not simply a gift to the child. The great short-story writer Grace Paley once sat next to me at a literary dinner, which is a memory I treasure, and she said to me warmly during a conversation about a novelist with an astonishingly long list of books, "Ah, Anna, think how prolific we would have been had we not had children." And she was right about that, but what I'm certain she knew was that we might have been less good at the work, because our children force us to relive the world in a way that can enrich the page. And because I am somehow more present on those occasions when I am with my grandson, precisely because I have less to do with his day-to-day maintenance, I am even more aware of this. Arthur squats to talk about the bumblebees; I respond with some musings on the failing willow tree. He says frogs say **gung;** I reply that snakes say **sssssss.** I say the things that long life has made me forget to say, or even to think. I wish I could do more of this in Mandarin, and we keep talking about resuming our lessons, which fills me with dread, since my head literally hurt when I did my homework, and even our lovely tutor seemed a bit taken aback by the tin ear implicit in my pronunciation. Maybe I will learn more, maybe not. In the meantime I'm speaking the nana language of love and hoping Arthur recognizes, if not every word, then all the tones.

# WE INTERRUPT THE WORKING WEEK FOR AN ARTHUR WEEKEND

We are sitting on the bench by a frog pond. I have been ordered to find and catch a frog, and have been a considerable disappointment. So we are just chatting, frogless, although I continue to keep my eyes peeled. So much of being a grandmother is imagined aggrandizement, hearing the words: "I will never forget when my nana plucked a frog from the reeds and handed it to me." It doesn't matter if you are a nana nurse / dentist / teacher / Supreme Court justice / neurosurgeon / CEO / MVP / you get the idea. Did you deliver the frog? Of course, later, when the frog is actually delivered, when Nana snags one and offers it held carefully in her fist, because the last thing she wants to produce is a dead frog, it will develop that Arthur doesn't really want to get up close and personal with it. One part of raising children is discovering the concept of their enormous desire for things it turns out they don't actually want except in theory. (Our daughter once ordered oysters in a restaurant when she was six. You can imagine how that turned out. Good thing her father and I both like oysters.) Spending time with kids winds up being a series of teachable moments . . . for you. As Arthur recoils from the reality of frog, we learn again that, young, old, or in between, much of what we think we yearn for loses its allure when it is in hand.

Not grandchildren, though.

Most of what I say are full sentences. Most of what Arthur says at this moment in time are phrases, some designed to trick me:

"A brown cow."

"A brown cow." (Why do we repeat everything they say? Is it to reinforce language or to seem companionable?)

"A black cow." One day he had a

meltdown because the cows at the farm down the road had ambled into a back field and were therefore not available. Why cows, the most boring of animals? Why not horses? Who can read the mind of a toddler? I had one child who was obsessed with snakes, then bats, later vampires. It's all a progression. Although I'm not exactly sure where we go from cows. Trucks?

"And a blue cow," Arthur says, looking at me searchingly.

"A blue cow?" I say, miming shock and amazement.

"Nooooooo," he says. He loves this, trolling Nana. Will she fall for it? Nooooooo. For some reason at this moment his "yes" and "no" are elongated and the vowels oddly shaped, so that he sounds vaguely Swedish. After a while you realize that most of us use language to communicate but that that's not always true of toddlers. They tend to roll the words around in their mouths like hard candy, repeat them over and over to show mastery. Arthur repeats words, but it's unclear which ones will stick, or are already stuck. We go down the road to the wildlife rehabilitation center, and he mimics us quite clearly. "Eagle." "Snake." "Porcupine." Will he remember "porcupine"? That seems like a boutique word, not necessary for everyday life.

One of his favorite words now is "Pop." There's no question that it feels good in his mouth, but it's not just that. In the way these things usually go in the house of family, Nana is wallpaper and Pop is a chandelier. "Pop! Pop!" he shouts now, searching for his grandfather. For a while, Pop's name was uttered in a whisper, like Maria in the **West Side Story** song: say it soft and it's almost like praying. Arthur suspects Pop's devotion makes him a soft touch. When Nana says no to donuts, Arthur cries, "I want Pop!"

It's instructive, to compare and contrast his last two summers here in the country. The first summer he was just a little nugget, lying on his back on a quilt on the lawn, looking up glassily into the tree canopy, subsisting on breast milk and fresh air. The signal event of that time for me was one day in the kitchen when, the dogs mobbing their water bowl, he laughed for no reason any of us could apprehend, a deep, rolling chortle that seemed as though it had emerged from a much bigger person, like Henry VIII. The double takes we all did! Where did it come from? What did it mean? What a mystery a baby is.

Last summer he was becoming a person, staggering across the same lawn, floating around the pool in some inflatable device with a big sun hat shading his little face. Many mornings he would go on my usual four-mile trek in his jogging stroller, his mother and I taking turns pushing, and on the rise where the valley lay spread before us like his kingdom we would purloin a half-grown ear from the cornfield and let him gnaw away, so that the stroller was always full of tiny niblets, white and glossy as baby teeth. It was the morning when I was pushing him solo that a black bear crossed the road some yards in front of me, triggering a primitive response that I suppose must at some level be purely chemical, the sensation built into all humans to protect their young. Not just humans, actually—look at the way a pair of geese will hiss if a dog tries to approach the goslings. I would have hissed had I had the time, but the bear merely toddled on, big and benign, without ever looking at my precious cargo or me.

If that happened during his third summer, Arthur would likely have pointed and said, "Bear." He knows bears from his books. Years from now he might take pictures of the bear to send to his friends, who are somewhere doing cool things that he is not because he has to spend the weekend with his grandparents. Now he happily has breakfast, sharing some yogurt, some oatmeal, even the occasional donut. Right now Arthur is a breakfast guy. You know that line about breakfast being the most important meal of the day? Arthur made that up, although no one but us could understand him. Stand by for his Nobel.

I know this may not last. I have been here before, and so I can envision it, a time when he may stay at our house as a teenager, the door to what was once his father's room and is now his closed for privacy, and rush out of the house as I toast

him an English muffin or fill a bowl with
a clatter of granola. Maybe he will grab his
own donut at the corner bodega, or a cup
of coffee with three sugars, because teenagers like the idea of coffee better than the
reality. "The most important meal of
the day!" I will shout after him. I hope I
will know not to be offended. I have been
here before. I know that the annoyance of
the early teens gives way to the companion-
ship of the late twenties. The progression is
so satisfying.

For us, some of the progression is
unseen. Most grandparents know their
grandchildren in what amount to snap-
shots. You see him on a Tuesday, and then
a week later he's back with ten additional
words and a new fascination with turtles or
fire trucks or his own feet. Sunday he's
fractious, Monday apparently a delightful
dream, when he's out of your sight but not
out of your mind. Except for those who
care for their grandchildren every day, we
don't see the continuous documentary loop
that parents do. "His language has grown
so much!" we say, delighted. "Look at how

he's holding the pencil!" A big part of our grandparent job is expressing ecstatic appreciation for everything from urination to reflexes. We must always silence the irritated voice of adult competency: Okay, I get it, I get it, you drew a 3. But, honestly, a 3 isn't that hard. A 5, now, there's a number. And this 3 doesn't even look that much like a 3.

No. It is the greatest 3 that anyone has ever drawn. Look at that 3!

As one of them I should note that the current crop of grandparents is a good news/bad news bunch. First of all, let us acknowledge that, like virtually everything else they've done, the baby boomers tend to act as though they've invented grandparenting. Certainly the size of our demographic has inflated the state. The census bureau says that in the year Arthur was born, there were more grandparents in the United States than ever before in our history, up by nearly 25 percent in the last two decades. At the same time, we are part of a funnel, the net effect of changing ideas about how many people reasonably constitute a family. My paternal grandfather had thirty-two grandchildren. His son, my father, had twelve. I don't know how many grandchildren we will eventually have—and that is not a hint, a directive, or a rebuke—but I can easily figure out that it would take some extraordinary act of either conception or adoption for me to come anywhere close to twelve.

Besides, I must admit that while I would welcome more, I treasure this time of JA— Just Arthur. My elder son was followed in quick succession by his brother, which was a very good thing in many ways, but it didn't leave much time for JQ—Just Quin. Someday perhaps there will be a cousin scrum, with Arthur leading it, but for right now it is just the two of us. Arthur is telling me a long, involved story about a turtle coming out from under the dock. I am getting maybe every third word, in part because his diction remains imprecise, in part because if he invented fire at the end of the dock I would not notice because I would be distracted by worrying about him falling into the pond. If he fell into the pond there would follow for many weeks a long, involved story about falling into the pond. There are these breathless "uh"s that punctuate every story at the moment, as though his mind is racing and neither his vocabulary nor his mouth can catch up with it: "And . . . uh . . . the turtle . . . swimming . . . and the bass . . . and the trout . . . and the turtle . . . uh . . . came out . . . uh . . . swimming . . ." Pop said the other day that Arthur is surely a storyteller, and I thrilled to the words, because of course that is what I am. But then I stopped and thought, no, don't do that. Let him find his own way. Let him realize that in our family, his family, the family business is not storytelling or law or anything but individuality.

"Let's go look at the bird's nest," I say, but he doesn't move, still crouched at the end of the dock. "Bass," he says authoritatively as a bass swims by, and then he begins the turtle story again.

# REVELATION

My elder son is the kind of guy who knows things. **Moby-Dick.** Marvel comics. Popular music. Chinese history. He's very precise in language and usage and one of the best-read people I've ever known. He does the last copyedit on the typeset manuscript of my novels, and he always manages to spot something that needs fixing. For Christmas I got him a T-shirt that says GRAMMAR POLICE: TO CORRECT AND SERVE. He wears it, too.

He has the ability to focus deeply in a way I do not, and while I am on the scattered side he is exceptionally good at detail work, perhaps to a fault: uncounted are the number of times I have quoted to him the adage "the perfect is the enemy of the good." When he wanted to get the entire family around the table to spring the news on us that he and his wife were expecting their first child, he did it by saying we needed to discuss estate planning. The fact that we all took him at his word tells you something about how methodical and mature he is.

And because of many of these traits, which are challenged by and even contrary to the chaos of life with a child, I am not sure I would have predicted how excellent a father he would turn out to be. There are many thrilling things about being a grandmother—who knew it would be so satisfying at my age to put my right foot in, to take my right foot out, to put my right foot in, and to shake it all about?—but for me one of the most thrilling is watching my eldest child be a first-rate parent. Conversely, men and women I've met who are raising their own grandchildren say that one of the hardest parts of their lives is not the school run or the sports games, chasing a Frisbee around the yard or laying down the law about lights-out. It's the constant distress about having raised a son or daughter who is unwilling or unable to be a good parent. When I see my son and Arthur at the school pickup, the man and the boy both with joyous smiles and arms outstretched, I can only conclude that Arthur's father is really good at this. I have to be honest and say I didn't entirely see that coming.

We have a trope in our family, about flowers and gardeners, those who expect to be cared for and those who do the caring. My second son is what you might call a master gardener, and I never doubted that he would find a way to become a father. (Although it turns out he can be surprisingly hardcore when the occasion demands; one evening he was minding Arthur in the midst of one of those toddler crying jags that is second cousin to demonic possession. "Arthur, breathe," his uncle commanded sternly, and Arthur did.) Our daughter started babysitting almost as soon as she was no longer the babysittee; several times she looked after infant twins, which is a temporarily effective form of contraception. Definitely future mom material.

But for the longest time our elder son said that he had no intention of filling the parental position, and for what was, as is his wont, a logical reason. He is a person who likes to do things that he knows he can do well—which may explain why he didn't walk until he was almost two—and he said it was too hard to do the job of fathering correctly and catastrophic to do it wrong. Who was I to argue? I, too, had intended in my twenties to go through life childless. I'd had to take some responsibility for my siblings after the death of our mother, and I'd not only found the task onerous and tedious, I'd become far too aware of the centrality of a mother to a family's existence and terrified of playing such a pivotal role in the lives of others. I was also the leading edge of those character traits that are in opposition to motherhood. I wasn't a fan of deferred gratification, and I wanted to do what I wanted to do when I wanted to do it. As the eldest of five, I grew up craving my own things: not shared, not divided up. The first time I went to a Chinese restaurant and realized that everyone else expected to dig in to the food I'd ordered was traumatic. Once I got my own place there were two things I couldn't wait to have: as much bacon as I wanted, and a batter bowl I could lick by myself. Do you know how little there is to lick off the wooden spoon when five children each get a lick?

When I was a teenager I read a book called **The Baby Trap,** by Ellen Peck. It seems unremarkable today, when people feel so much freer to choose whether to have children or not, but at the time it was revolutionary to me, to read these words: "Take your pick. One or the other. Housework and children—or the glamour, involvement and excitement of a full life."

That's your pick? Come on, I was nineteen. That's an easy choice when you're nineteen and your other guidepost is Ayn Rand's **The Fountainhead**, which suggests that altruism is a trap and self-interest should be your ruling principle. I was totally Team Anna, and remained so for some time. And then one day something shifted. I cannot say why, and I do not pretend to think that people who remain childless are selfish or wrong and that at some point they will rue their decision, which they must get so very tired of hearing. Quite the contrary: the fact is I've known some people who had children over the years who should have thought better of that decision, and when I meet a couple who are childless by choice (as opposed to the many who are childless because sometimes nature is cruel), I don't think they are shortsighted, stupid, or selfish. Being a parent is an awesome responsibility, and I believe it should be freely chosen and that it is not for everyone. But after years of saying I would never do it, eventually I chose it and managed to embrace what swiftly became the most transformative experience of my life.

But sometimes now I remember what I once felt like, what once led me to **The Baby Trap** and Ayn Rand, whose novels my father recommended because he thought they would show me the error of my egocentric ways. (My father was a very smart man, but to say he didn't understand the mind of a teenage girl is an understatement.) At a threshold level, one of the challenges in becoming a grandparent is that, over time, as our children grow into lives of their own, we revert to that Me Me place.

You get used to having an orderly house, and then suddenly you don't, at least not if your grandchildren are going to feel welcome. They have to be able to scatter the Legos, leave a rubber T. rex on the kitchen counter or a bathing suit on the bathroom floor. You get used to wearing white pants without fear, and then there are those grass stains from sitting on the lawn or the drool blot left over from a teething baby. You get used to being able to do what you want, and then you're back on the clock, your schedule synchronized with naps or school pickups or camp visiting days.

You have finally gotten to the point where you no longer have to share: time, space, ice cream, clothes. Place the pillows carefully on the couch, and a week later the pillows are where you left them. Unless you have grandchildren. There are some people who want untrammeled pillows, who decide that their sharing days are done. They don't want cocoa or crayons in their living rooms. Although what is the point of maturity if you haven't learned that a pristine living room is not the secret of life?

I remember why I didn't want to have children. It's just that the woman who felt that, who was intent on leading that life, is no longer me. I see my own experience so clearly mirrored in Quin's. He, too, came around for mysterious reasons after years of saying the job of father was not for him. He was wise enough to know that those men who accede to fatherhood because their wives want children, with the proviso that it's her job, have just made a fool's bargain, not for themselves but for their kids. He wholeheartedly embraced the challenge and the role; in the way he has done other things, his **no no no** became a **yes,** and a **yes** it has remained, in the best possible way. It is not simply that he took out a life-insurance policy and opened a college savings account; he opened his heart, as well, in ways he says he could not have imagined. The rigors of parenthood sometimes excavate the sentimental in the rationalist as well as the disciplinarian in the laissez-faire. We become an unexpected expanded version of ourselves.

Becoming a parent changed and enlarged my son; it's no stretch at all to say that parenthood made us both better people. I've watched him be a father to my grandson, and I've been thrilled by his ability to put his own concerns and needs aside to minister to those of this little boy, to put himself in the place time after time where he is attuned to who his son is and what he needs, whether indulgence or discipline. The same deep curiosity he brought to the work of Joseph Conrad or the Beijing Olympics he has brought to understanding Arthur down to the ground. He has plumbed stores of patience he never knew he had: I can't count how many times he has drawn Ferdinand the bull in chalk on the patio. But I know he will keep doing it until Arthur stops asking. He even created infant doggerel:

Arthur is the best,
Forget about the rest,
We put them to the test,
And Arthur is the best.
He loves his mother's breast
And impresses every guest.

**Our family is blessed**
**Because Arthur is the best.**

Being an oldest child often means you always feel like the adult in the room. Having Arthur has helped excavate Quin's inner kid. A person who does not suffer fools gladly, he has become uncommonly understanding. A person whose imagination can sometimes be leavened with skepticism, he is most often now joyful. A demanding person, he has become something of a softy. When the decision was made that Arthur was miserable from lack of sleep and that sleep training was in order, his parents repaired to their own quarters at our house, there to let their son cry it out. I texted to ask how things were going. **Ten minutes in Quin started to cry,** Lynn replied. **We have to wait until he's away for work.** When he was, Mama and Nana sat in the kitchen, the monitor turned to mute. "It's so good he's not here," Lynn said of her husband.

I was in an interview some time ago when an applicant said, "How would success be measured in this job? What would it look like five years in?" Being a parent is complicated; we fail every day in small ways and wait for the big reveal of adulthood to tell us whether we have ultimately succeeded.

Along the way there are various measurements, but they tend to be logistical, not spiritual. He wears underpants instead of diapers. She can write her name with a pencil. The grades are good. The diploma is in hand. They don't really tell the story, of course; they are guideposts, no more. Some people measure their success by the profession their children have chosen, by the purchase of a house, by how often they visit or call. But the only measurement, truly, is something that's quite subjective: have you raised good people?

I haven't decided yet if there are ways to measure being a successful grandparent. After all, the grades and the diploma are not precisely your purview. Some people try to salve their uncertainty by placing themselves in competition with the other grandparents. Some make the mistake of trying to subvert the ambiguity by doling stuff out, ever-larger and more-expensive toys and consumer electronics, ever-more-elaborate vacations. These grandparents wind up being the next-generation version of a divorced dad who only gets weekends, and so constructs some Potemkin village of late-night pizza and trips to all-inclusive resorts to make up for missing the boring, essential everyday. Believe me when I say, this is not a good look.

Because success is never measured by the satisfaction on an adolescent's face when he opens a new tech gadget. The greatest measures are more amorphous. There are small moments as a parent when you suddenly have reason to say to yourself, my God, it was all worth it, the sleepless nights because of stomach flu or broken curfews, the craziness around toilet training and SAT tests, the exhaustion and the worries and the second-guessing.

And then there are the moments that are like lightning striking, like sunrise and sunset and New Year's Eve all at once. I had one of those moments when I asked Quin what surprised him most about being a father. And he said, "I guess it's how much I love him in a way I've never loved anyone before."

And, ladies and gentlemen, my work here is done.

## SMALL MOMENTS

The evening routine is almost done. Arthur has had dinner, sweet potato and chicken sausage. He stayed in the bath for a long time, blinked and gasped dramatically as his hair was washed, ran naked down the hall once he was dried. Getting him into his pajamas should be an Olympic sport. He thinks the struggle is hilarious.

Finally we have settled into the rocker in his room to read, and I realize that I have forgotten my reading glasses. They were once a convenience and are now a necessity. But luckily there is a book by the chair that I do not need to be able to see, because I can recite it from memory, so I pick it up and put my arm around my grandson and begin:

"In the great green room . . ."

"Mouse," Arthur says.

"There is a mouse," I say.

Is there anything better than sitting in a rocking chair with a little boy next to you while you read him **Goodnight Moon?** Is there anything more magical than the connection between reader and book, Nana reading and grandson listening? Arthur discovered the book **The Story of Ferdinand,** and because of the gentle bull, he is interested in both flowers and bumblebees. I assume he is learning lessons about the possibility of being both strong and gentle, but who knows? All I know is that books are magic. **The Story of Ferdinand** was published when my father was seven years old, and yet here is his great-grandson attending as Ferdinand is taken to the bull-ring and refuses to fight.

Some of the books Arthur reads have moved from shelves in our home to the ones in his. A shared language, a shared past. The copy of **Quack! Quack!** is a bit furred at the edges. His **Ferdinand** is new, and his **Goodnight Moon** and his **Shrek**, but he has our old copy of **An Illustrated History of Dinosaurs** and **Hey, Al**. He got a lot of books before he was born, at the baby shower, and then more for each successive birthday. He has a Nana book, and a **Llama Llama** book about spending the night at your grandparents'. I didn't know those books before, but I'm glad they, and others like them, exist.

"Goodnight light and the red balloon," I read, or, more accurately, recite.

Arthur leans in. "The bears," he says.

Through my own reading I learned, when my boys were small, that psychological theory had it that to become adult men they would have to separate convincingly from me, break the bonds that attached them to the person from whence they came, the person whom many of us consider the center of our psyche. But because they were boys, that bond could not stand if they were to reach maturity.

I don't want to get into a tussle with Sigmund Freud here, who is a much bigger

name than I am, but I considered this
a blunt object of personal development,
cruel and unnecessary, perhaps the root of
the problem so many men have with emotional intimacy. My boys loved me so,
and yet at a certain point the prevailing
culture insisted that they should reject me?
Ridiculous, and completely unacceptable,
for their sakes as much as mine.

So I turned where I had so many times
over the course of my life, to books. I
transmuted our connection into that of
readers and writers. We talked about so
many things, connected over and over
again, over characterization, description,
theme. But most of the time we were talking about ourselves. Because that's one of
the really important things about books,
that they enable you to talk to your children about all sorts of things, sometimes
without speaking at all.

"And goodnight to the old lady whisper-
ing 'hush,'" I say to Arthur, pretending to
read although I am really remembering,
falling down the well of memory as I speak,
other children, other chairs.

Arthur will begin to forget his nana as a pillow for his head, an encircling arm, a low voice intoning, "In the great green room." He will begin to see her as an old woman with her life behind her who he might conclude has nothing in common with a young man just figuring it all out. And to combat that I will try to read the books he's reading, and I will talk to him about them, which will really be talking to him about himself.

"Goodnight noises everywhere," I say finally.

"Another book," Arthur says, and how can I say no?

Lessons learned:

- Have a pair of glasses handy.

- If not, there's **Green Eggs and Ham.** Or **In the Night Kitchen.**

- Reading connects us. Always and forever.

# THE VILLAGE

Parenting has changed a great deal over the last century. For one thing, it wasn't even called parenting until recently; people of my parents' generation had babies and then got on with it. Stimulation consisted largely of saying, "Go outside and play," and an educational toy was your younger sibling. Shoes were often hand-me-downs, and parochial school uniforms certainly were. The teacher was always right, especially if she happened to be a nun; the idea that our mothers would check our homework, much less march into the school building and confront Sister Mary Luke over a math test, was unthinkable.

Some years ago my friend Donna and I were reminiscing about pushing our baby sisters, who were born within weeks of one another, in their strollers at the request of our mothers. We basically parked the girls and went about our business. "Did we even put the brake on the stroller?" Donna asked. "There was a brake?" I said.

It was like that then.

The dads were available to turn down requests for money and to tell what I now suspect were apocryphal stories about the hardships of their own early lives. So-called homemaking was the territory of women alone. My father could cook two things when I was a kid: grilled cheese sandwiches and tomato soup. (Campbell's, from a can, so not exactly culinary legerdemain. Although the man made a mean grilled cheese sandwich, largely because he put so much butter in the pan that it essentially constituted deep-fat frying.) This was the meal he made whenever my mother was in the hospital having another baby, the only time when he was home during a weekday.

On the other hand, my mother's life went

like this: pregnant, baby; pregnant, toddler/
baby; pregnant, child/toddler/baby; pregnant, child/child/toddler/baby; pregnant,
child/child/child/toddler/baby. Totally un-
fair that by the time she'd reached teen/teen/
teen/child/child, she died. If I ever get a
chance to talk to her again, I would say so
many things, but one of them would be,
jeez Louise, how the hell did you do it?

But parenting was different then, less
crazy and manic, and of necessity five children meant a different kind of attention and
concentration. This meant grandparenting
was different, as well. To repeat, because it
deserves repetition: my paternal grandparents had thirty-two grandchildren. (I
double-checked. When you have that many
cousins, sometimes you lose track, but
thirty-two is accurate.) In the year my sister
was born, four other cousins arrived as well.
This wasn't as aberrational as current standards make it sound. Most families in my
grandparents' orbit and in our neighborhood had something similar going on: in
really large families, with one priest and
one nun and one daughter who was the

sacrificial lamb fated never to marry so she could care for her aged parents, you were still bound to have a sizable next generation. I took all this for granted until the time, some years ago, when I was discussing it with an old friend whose family was twice as large as my own. "There was just never enough," she said, which I found puzzling since her family had been prosperous, but she shook her head. "Enough time, enough attention. You just can't pay enough attention to that many kids." Which makes perfect sense under the new rules, in which I was always trying to individuate, doing things alone with each of my three in turn. To her credit, our mother tried to do the same, to break each of us out from the crowd of "the kids." But it was hard and often didn't happen.

Not only was that true, no one felt badly about it. The motto "It takes a village" means, among other things, that your own mother and father simply won't have the time to do all the raising, and conventional wisdom has it that the slack was taken up by aunts, uncles, neighbors, and, of course, grandparents. But that last didn't seem accurate when I was a child. My grandparents were not particularly engaged or attentive, although we were taken to see them ritualistically, more for obeisance than face time, always on Sundays, as though it were an extension of the morning's religious rites. Their grandparenting matched the style of their parenting, so different from today's, replete with advice books, mommy blogs, online forums for everything from breastfeeding to sex roles. My grandparents seem to have believed that their role was to house, clothe, and feed children who would then do the same for their own. The current assumption of unconditional love would have been ridiculous to them. Love was purely conditional, on what you accomplished, on who you became, on how you behaved. Love needed to be earned. Otherwise, of what value was it?

My grandparents looked like old people. Kitty had silver hair and Cuban heels. Gene had spectacles and a considerable waistline. Concetta wore shapeless dresses of indiscriminate color, and no makeup. Caesar tended his tomato plants in dress shirts and sharp shark-skin slacks. It would never have occurred to any of them to get down on the floor with us, and, not to be mean, but I'm not sure they could have gotten back up again if they had. Children played and tried not to bother any-one. Adults had cocktails and talked among themselves. You could interrupt to tell them one of your cousins had broken a leg in the backyard, and you might still get in trouble for interrupting. If my grandparents ever babysat for us, I have absolutely no memory of it. Why would they? Our mothers never went anywhere, and if they did, we could be dropped off with Aunt Joan or Aunt Gloria.

My grandmother and grandfather Quindlen were both children of large Irish families, who produced such a family them-selves and expected their own children to do so. The continuation of their line was taken for granted: there would be Quindlens into perpetuity. They would be Catholic and, of course, Caucasian. And yet, in this new world, here we are with a grandson neither Catholic nor Caucasian. He will never have dozens of cousins, and in some ways he doesn't need to: as families have grown smaller and more far-flung, most young people have created a family of friends. While in my extended family we had a rotating cadre of aunt and uncle godparents, today my younger son is the godfather to my best friend's son's little girl.

The numbers make this a necessity, and grandchildren a different sort of gift. Some of our friends had just one child, and in an age of falling birth rates that may mean no grandchildren or perhaps just one. This is a marked change in the landscape of life. A friend of my daughter's once said at our dining room table that he was an only child, and my father acted as though he were a unicorn. Do the math: the only way in which my paternal grandparents would have had no grandchildren was if the planet had been wiped out by an asteroid.

My father used to call me almost every morning, usually to discuss some relatively obscure book he was reading. A typical opening gambit went like this: "How much do you know about Charlemagne, baby?" Then he was off to the races. But one day he said, breathlessly, "Did you see **Nova** last night? Unbelievable. They showed a baby being born. I'll tell you, I was moved. Really moved. I cried. It was really something."

The man had five children and had never seen a baby being born until he watched it on public television.

It's not that being a grandparent today is better or worse, it's just different. Since baby boomers will live so much longer than past generations, many children will have grandparents far longer than I did, and those grandparents will be more active, more likely to take them skiing than to sit at the kitchen table and quiz them about their last report card. People are always surprised to hear that the average age of a grandmother at the moment is around fifty. That's because, when life expectancy rarely breached seventy, fifty seemed old; today, with more people than ever before reaching ninety, fifty seems young.

Baby-boomer grandparents will seem both older and younger than their predecessors. Older, because many of them are—a rise in the age of childbearing means that,

while the average age of becoming a grandparent is fifty for a woman, those women
who waited until their late thirties to have
children and who have children who are
doing the same may not become grandmothers for the first time until they are in
their seventies. (I recently chatted with a
new mom whose daughter has two sets of
grandparents, one pair sixty-four, the other
eighty-one.) Younger, too, because in a society in which a high school student and her
grandmother may wear the same kind of
jeans and the same T-shirt, and in which
there is an 80–89 age group in the New York
City Marathon, the age of the cozy cookie-
jar grandmother is skidding to a close in
many households. Our grandmothers were
pre-gym, pre-Botox, pre–skinny jeans.

I was sixty-four when Arthur was born,
as opposed to my grandmother Quindlen,
who was forty-seven when her first grandchild arrived. But I daresay that in many
ways I seemed younger than she did then, in
how I looked and in how I lived. One of my
most comical nana moments came waiting
to order fish at a gourmet market on the

West Side of Manhattan, with Arthur in a sling on my chest. I was kissing his head and murmuring nonsense and waiting for tuna steaks when the woman next to me said, "You look great. For how young he is." It took me a moment to realize that she was suggesting I was the baby's mother. Now, I look okay for my age, but no one is going to mistake me for a thirty-five-year-old, not by a long shot. But I realized that there are in fact women closer to my age than that of my daughter-in-law who, by virtue of medical intervention, have children, and that maybe I had momentarily been mistaken for one such. Today's forty-seven-year-old could be a much older mother or a youngish grandmother. It's a sea change.

But some parts of being a grandparent haven't changed much, because grandchildren still want some of the same things they've always wanted. They still want to eat cookie dough before the cookies are baked, to come down the sliding board backward, to bounce on the bed even if they know it's forbidden, and to jump out from behind the door and say "Boo!" and have you act as though you're shocked and terrified. Sidewalk chalk, bubbles: those still entertain. For how long have grandfathers been pretending to take your nose by pushing the pad of their thumb through their first two fingers? My father did it to my kids. Even my stolid grandfather did it to me, although his manner probably made me genuinely believe not only that he actually had taken my nose but that he was unlikely to return it without good reason.

At age two, Arthur loves it when Pop takes his nose. At age five he will play along but insist that it's not his nose at all. "That's your thumb," he may say accusatorily, as so many have done before him. In Nanaville a two-year-old finds almost anything weird entertaining and, often, hilarious. As he ages, he will become more jaded. A five-year-old cares if you are fun, a teenager that you are cool. You want your parents to be leached of all eccentricity, but it's acceptable to have a quirky grandparent (although not too quirky). I remember one of my kids at the end of Grandparents' Day at school saying, "Everybody thought Grandpop was funny." Gold star for Grandpop.

I didn't think my grandfathers were funny. I thought they were the patriarchs, the source of all judgment and wisdom. I don't think either of them ever hugged or kissed me, ever praised me or said they loved me. Yet I knew that they did, even without words. I suppose that particular patriarchy is done, and in the main that's a good thing. It is better to hug, to kiss, to praise. But it makes me wonder how our grandchildren will place us in this new world. For those of us who had a more egalitarian, less arm's-length relationship with our children, it may be inevitable that our grandkids will see us less as towering figures and more as demi-parents, who pick them up at school when their parents are not available, who trail around the county fair behind Mom and Dad, waiting to be asked for a waffle ice cream sandwich or a roll of tickets for the rides. My grandparents did not do county fairs. They weren't even interested in hearing about them. Sometimes I wonder now: once all of us were born, could they tell you all thirty-two names? Perhaps that's beside the point. In their time they were not having grandchildren so much as building a clan.

# DID THEY ASK YOU?

I'm not going to go into too much detail here, because most of it reflects badly on me. Let's just say that two very thoughtful and caring human beings made the decision, after their first sitter went back to China, to handle childcare by sending their son to something they referred to as a preschool. This very much upset the little boy's grandparents, who felt that their grandson was far too young for such an arrangement. One of the grandparents—let's say the nana, since the pop was upset but wasn't going to say a word except to the nana— said something. Well, maybe more than one something. Maybe several things.

At which point her son, who had rarely done so before, pushed back. Hard. He was not rude or mean-spirited, but it was clear he wanted his mother to back off. And so back off she did.

So the next morning the nana—let's call her, for the sake of argument, me—was out for her morning walk with her friend Susan, whom she considers a source of all sensible insights and who once taught the nana's sons in elementary school. Susan's last name is Parent. You can't make this stuff up. So I recount this entire chain of events, and at the end there is a silence so loud that you can hear the birds singing in the trees. And then Susan says, not at all unkindly, "Did they ask you?"

Have you ever had one of those moments when you hear something that you think you should cross-stitch on a sampler or format in a continuous digital loop across the bottom of your computer screen?

This was one of those moments: Did they ask you for your opinion? Did they want to know what you thought, whether you approved or not? Or did you proffer your unsolicited advice and considered judgment, which, in the case of child and parent, inevitably sounds like Mother Knows Best?

This moment reverberates in my head continuously, and I hope it will do so forever, because it marks a moment when I truly got nana religion. Did they ask you? When our grandson is throwing a fit and his parents are dealing with it. When he has a slight temperature and is cranky. When he wants to go in the pool, doesn't want to go to the potty, wants a cookie, doesn't want peas. I have opinions on all of those things to a greater or lesser extent. That boy is crabby. That boy is sick. He needs Motrin. He needs a good talking-to, a good night's sleep. A veteran of motherhood often talks in declarative sentences. That baby is tired. That baby is hungry. How odd that the addled parents of years past become so certain of so much when they are a generation removed. How odd, and how dangerous, to talk as though your words are on stone tablets. Nana judgment must be employed judiciously, and exercised carefully. Be warned: those who make their opinions sound like the Ten Commandments see their grandchildren only on major holidays and in photographs.

There are really only two commandments of Nanaville: love the grandchildren, and hold your tongue.

I am sad to say that the grandparents who do otherwise are the ones about which we tend to hear most often, that great Greek chorus that says, mine were out of diapers by age two, how come he isn't talking yet, and, later on, I don't like those friends of hers, why did you let her do that to her hair, what kind of wedding is that? Many human relations are about power and control at base, but the grandparents who try to exercise that power and exert that control do so at their peril, especially with parents who may already be feeling frazzled and unsure. Which, as far as I've been able to tell, is most parents much of the time.

Being a good grandparent requires you to bring the past to the table and then let go of it in the face of change. It is easy to feel defensive if your son or daughter is doing things differently than you did, as though the differences are a rebuke. But so much of the change our children exemplify is change for the better, in ways large and small. So much good stuff has been invented since I was last doing this, starting with maternity clothes that don't look like a floral hot-air balloon. It is almost impossible to try to communicate the vast improvements in breast pumps, particularly once you've actually witnessed a young woman wearing one that attaches to a sports bra and fills two plastic freezer pouches at once in the time it takes her to send a couple of business emails. I never used one, since those that existed when I was nursing took the length of a television drama to give you some sad ounces at the bottom of a bottle.

Then there is the car seat. As I looked at its construction, which appears to have been undertaken by NASA, and its installation, which initially stymied two highly intelligent college graduates, all I could think was that every time they were in a moving car, my own children were in imminent danger of death. And these were the kids we thought we were protecting so diligently, given that as toddlers many of us were bouncing around in the back of a station wagon, without seat belts because there was no such thing as seat belts.

The temptation is to see these shifts and to push back against them. Don't. Just don't. Each generation inevitably gets better stuff, and some of it is prime.

One of my favorites is the monitor that is in Arthur's room. It is video as well as audio, and you can get the signal on any device. Which means that one of my favorite things to do—while reading in bed at night, waking at dawn to make the coffee, or even when across the country, me in a West Coast hotel room, he asleep in New York City—is to check in on Arthur. Sometimes he's lying on his back, one leg bent at the knee, a foot held on a slat. I don't know how he sleeps like that. Sometimes he's in a far corner, outside camera range, and I have to listen closely for his breathing. Occasionally I catch him newly awake: "Hello?" he calls. "Hello?" I love that. Every once in a while I hear one of his parents reply from the kitchen next door, and then

I shut the camera down. I have rules for myself: as soon as the parents can be heard or seen, I am so out of there. I only watch when Arthur is alone. It is always infinitely more entertaining than reality television. One day I tuned in to a spirited rendition of "Old MacDonald Had a Farm." There was a moo moo here and a moo moo there. "Ee i ee i ooooooooh," he sang loudly. I listened for a long time.

I suppose if you were being literal you could consider this cyberstalking.

What a balancing act this is, in some ways unparalleled in the annals of parenting. Arthur's other grandparents live a world away; how thrilling it is to see him, sitting in front of an iPad, talking to them on WeChat. Technology is a wonderful way to narrow the distance between grandparents and grandchildren when people live elsewhere. You couldn't do that in the good old days.

I'm not a fan of the so-called good old days. It seems to me obvious that our grandchildren will grow up in a fairer and, in some ways, more interesting world than we did. We will tell them the stories, of how a telephone was once anchored to the wall and had a cord attached to it, of how watching a specific program required you to be in front of a television at a specific time. What's that, Nana, they will say, looking at the small round scar on my upper arm, and I will say, there was a disease called smallpox and we all got inoculated against it but then it was gone and you didn't need to get one of these anymore. Now you get inoculated against chicken pox instead. But when your daddy was little they didn't have that vaccine yet, and so your daddy and your uncle and your aunt all got chicken pox around the same time, and we spent several summer days in oatmeal baths. These are the kinds of things grandparents are built for and invaluable at. Research shows that one of the most useful functions of grandparents is to transmit stories, to reflect a personal history that enriches children's sense of the world as it once was. Although I have to admit, when I was young I got a little tired of those Great Depression stories. Were they really that excited about getting an orange in their stockings at Christmas?

No question that some of the progress with which our children have grown to adulthood and then parenthood comes with substantial pitfalls. It was bad enough a century ago to have your mother living in the house next door (or the room next door), getting on your case about indulging the child or not indulging the child, having your aunts stopping by to opine on your mothering skills or lack of same. But today there is also a great faceless mob of strangers passing judgment, in magazines and newspapers, on television programs and online, saying that you haven't breastfed long enough, that you haven't chosen the right preschool, that you haven't handled sibling rivalry or stranger anxiety or Oedipal transference properly. There are so many people giving young parents conflicting information and telling them that they are botching what they understand is the most important job they will ever have. They certainly don't need Nana adding to the din. If anything, they need you telling them to ignore the naysayers and follow their gut.

I appreciate that this is difficult, that having done the job of parent in a satisfactory way there is the temptation to simply try to sidle into the slot again. There's a knee-jerk response that so many of us can't help having, like this, a Christmas ago, my eyes aglow, my lists at the ready:

Hooray! I finally get to be Santa again!

Mom, I'm Santa.

Da-dum-**dum**.

The flip side, of course, is that we grandparents feel responsibility without true authority, which is an uncomfortable place to be. (It's also the place where teenagers most often find themselves, which is why I've always been hugely sympathetic to adolescents.) I think of this most often when I pass a large building near our home in the city, a place where a terrible tragedy occurred. A residence for older adults, it has benches facing the street outside, and a woman was sitting on one of those benches with her two-year-old granddaughter when a piece of the brick façade fell and hit them. The grandmother was injured. The child died. I never walk past without thinking of the two of them, and of the little girl's parents, but I can't think too hard or too long. I also never walk on that side of the street when I have Arthur with me. This is silly, of course. It's probably one of the safest places in the city, right? After something like that, the owners probably go over the façade with a magnifying glass. And I tell myself that, but I still cross over with the stroller.

Do you know how deer care for their newborns? They leave them so that they will be less likely to draw predators. A doe returns to her baby to nurse and to eat its droppings so odors won't attract danger. One of the mistakes well-meaning humans make all the time is to find a fawn curled into a spotted pillow in a field and think it's been abandoned, when in truth its mother has evidenced a deep instinctive notion of how to keep her offspring safe until it is better able to fend for itself.

And yet danger is sometimes inevitable. Our beloved dog, responding to millennia of instinct, once picked up a fawn from the tall grass as it screamed. From nowhere a doe appeared, rearing, running, circling. I will never forget her wild eyes or the sound her baby made before we persuaded the dog to back off. The impulse to protect the young from harm is primal; it's why strangers stand below the windows of burning buildings and hold out their arms for a child. But open arms and enormous care don't always forestall disaster. Bad things happen to little people.

I only had the usual garden-variety share of panic-stricken blips. The babies fell off the bed. The children got illnesses of various types. Maria leapt from the sofa and broke her arm. Quin fell in the tub, Chris nicked his forehead, and both of them got stitches. Some of these occasions were educational: a doctor said that a significant number of men have a scar just beneath their chin from when they hit it just the same way Quin did, and another told me that you don't need to make a fuss about a plastic surgeon if the line of a small wound runs with the grain of the skin, as Christopher's had. At the sight of blood, I did my best to stay chill, for their sakes as well as my own.

I could not be at all chill if anything happened to Arthur on my watch. The issue would not be dealing with the aftermath, the cut or the bruise. I can do those things in my sleep. It would be explaining to my son and his wife what had happened, seeing a scraped knee as evidence of my own carelessness. "Accidents happen," I used to tell the kids all the time when the accidents were theirs. But now? I try not to be hypervigilant with my grandson: that way lies those poor kids who are afraid of everything. He's pretty fearless, so we let him ride in the canoe (wearing a flotation device) and jump in the pool (with swimmies on his arms and an adult on each side). When he decided he'd had enough of sleeping in the crib, he managed to climb out, which gave me a day of palpitations, but his father, watching him on the monitor, described him as "reassuringly acrobatic in his escape." So I calmed down.

Arthur had one preschool teacher whose

approach set a template that suits me fine: one day at our house he fell, and as I waited for a wail, he picked himself up, threw his hands in the air, and said, "Ay yi yi!" Lord knows I'm glad we've reached the point at which we don't call kids crybabies or sissies anymore, but part of teaching them to be fully human is a sense of proportion. Some tumbles really, really hurt, and others are just ay yi yi. But, please, let's keep all tumbles to a minimum on my watch. A nana accident doesn't feel so much like an accident as like a betrayal of trust.

Luckily, Arthur's parents are a relaxed pair, his mother apt to say, "You're okay," when he takes a small bump or fall. And that's my attitude, too, so that I am not tempted to rush in with my take on the situation, to opine when I have not been asked for my opinion. I know that if Arthur's parents and I weren't so much on the same page about what's good for kids, it would be materially harder to keep my counsel. And there are many occasions on which they do actively seek it. I'm also grateful that the occasion on which I got my comeuppance came early on. I think making mistakes early, about things not quite so important on the great continuum, is an invaluable learning tool. And of course this entire nana thing is an education.

Let me state for the record about pre-school, about my reservations and their decision: I was completely wrong. I know it. I acknowledge it. I learned from it. Arthur loves preschool and has thrived there. On the mornings when I take him, he runs in to see his friends. He has grown so much. And so have I. I have strong opinions. Ask and you shall receive some useful version of them. Otherwise, I will try to be as quiet as the house at naptime.

# SMALL MOMENTS

The parents are away at a weekend wedding in Minneapolis, and Pop has a work commitment, so it is just Arthur and Nana, alone in the country.

When I heard him on the monitor, chattering to himself as the light seeped around the edges of the shades in his room here, I hurried over. He seemed delighted to see me, although he did look hopeful and say, "Dada?" as we crossed the drive later.

We did a long walk, he in the jogging stroller, me breathing heavy on the hills, and then we threw a ball for the dog for a while. We drove to the historical farm for the crafts fair, and I was glad I'd given him scrambled eggs and yogurt for breakfast as we sat facing one another, eating some baked goods with pecans and frosting that seemed to be made solely from the three essential food groups: butter, flour, and sugar. Not for the first time, I thanked God that neither of his parents were crazy people about stepping outside the nutritional lines. I still burn at the memory of handing back a little girl to her mother after I somehow had been saddled with her for the day, along with my own three. Four had been a lot, it had begun to rain hard, and I had run out of steam and into the indoor playground at McDonald's. When I mentioned that the little girl had had a Happy Meal with a small Sprite—no caffeine!— her mother said, her face as still as a snapshot, "She's never had sugar before."

Arthur has had sugar. He was breastfed for months, and his diet is heavy on fruit and vegetables and hummus and suchlike. Chinese dumplings, too, which are another important food group. But he has been known to have a cookie and like it, because it's too soon to tell who exactly he will be but he's clearly no dummy. If he had a cookie and didn't, I would be seriously worried.

The crafts fair is less exciting than it sounds. Arthur has no interest in handmade belts or pottery planters or dangly silver earrings, but he goes on a hayride, and he is intensely interested in the horses and the geese, which I steer him away from because geese are nasty. One attacked my second son when he was small. "Bad, bad goose!" he had said that day, knitting his nearly invisible blond brows. A man dressed up in period farmer garb put a baby goat in Arthur's lap, which I thought would be a wonderful moment, but he looked up at me as though to say, "What the heck is this?" so the man took it away and offered it to a slightly older child.

"Goat," Arthur said in the car, or something like it. So at least there was that.

Home for a nap after a diaper change and a wipe of sticky hands, and then a toddle around the back paths to the pool. The two of us took off our shoes and sat side by side on the long top step with our feet in the water and chatted, as one does, which in the case of a toddler means you talking a lot about various subjects, stopping while the toddler repeats a few words, intelligibly or not, and then adds a few things that sound more or less like something. Then the nana nods and says, "I know," or "That's right." It's not exactly a conversation in the conventional sense, but it passes the time.

It was very warm, and it had been a tiring day, because every day with a toddler is tiring, and so it took me a bit by surprise when Arthur, in a single movement, rose to his little unmarked feet on the step and launched himself into the pool. My first thought was that both of us were fully dressed and it would have been so much better if we'd been in bathing suits, and also that I was wearing a watch. It seems like every single time I've had to go into the water after a child I've been wearing a watch.

Of course, I am making all of this sound like it happened over time, when it happened in the time it takes a nana to dive into the pool, fully clothed, and pull a small boy to the surface, sputtering and gasping and crying for only a minute before he says, "Wet! Wet!" over and over again, even as he is wrapped in a beach towel, stripped naked, and set down on the grass.

Wow, the way a disposable diaper inflates when it's sodden is really something to see, even with these new thinner disposables. I knew that, of course. I was once staying with a friend at her in-laws' condo complex in Palm Beach, and my little boy fell into the pool with his diaper on, which immediately took on the contours of a flotation device. Ah, if only it had been. Some person of stature there sent a warning letter to the in-laws, saying that we had violated pool policy by allowing into the water a child clad in a diaper. I wondered then if they also had a policy against drowning.

We have no policy against diapers in the pool. However, we absolutely forbid toddlers to sink below its surface, eyes wide. The little ones always go down with eyes wide, although I suspect no wider than my

own as I watch in that instant before I
dive in.

"Wet!" Arthur says, running down the
slate path as I run after him, his butt dim-
pled as an orange.

Lessons learned:

- We probably should have started
  baby swim with him earlier.

- Maybe turn on the pool heater?

- Be ready, self, because no matter
  what happens—coyotes, mean
  bigger kids, thunderstorms,
  carnival rides—you are going to do
  whatever needs to be done to keep
  this boy safe and happy. Yes, I did
  say "carnival rides." I hate carnival
  rides, was forced onto a Ferris
  wheel several years ago by my
  whole family in an act of conspicuous cruelty and spent the entire
  time with my hands clamped on
  the safety bar and my eyes closed
  while my children laughed and

made their cars sway back and forth. "Look at the view!" they shouted.

But if it's just a grandchild and me at the county fair and that grandchild wants to go on the Tilt-A-Whirl, will I say, "Nana is terrified of the Tilt-A-Whirl, sweetheart"?

I will suck it up. I will dive in. Lesson learned.

# NONO'S

It was easy for me to become Nana, at least in terms of title. You just take the letters of my first name and scramble them. In a similar fashion my friend Ronnie became Nonnie. Why complicate things for little people? Of course, sometimes little people have their own ideas. My friend Binky intended to be called Nonna but is now Nini because that's what her grandson started calling her and she wasn't about to correct him. Although, come to think of it, a child could easily call a grandmother Binky, except that they might confuse their grandmother and their pacifier.

I hope my grandchildren all see me as a pacifier.

According to Etsy, where the stock of nana swag is enormous, there are grandmothers called Oma, Maw Maw, Mimi, Gigi, Bibi, and the really pretentious Funma. (If you're actually that much fun, it seems to me you don't have to advertise it.) In Yiddish there's Bubbe and Zayde; in Filipino, Lola and Lolo.

It was a great relief to discover that my Chinese name was almost the same as my English one. There is no question about what Chinese grandparents are called; as with so many other words in Mandarin, the terms carry freight apart from their most obvious meaning. Nainai is the term for paternal grandmother. Maternal grandmother is Laolao. The grandfathers have different names depending upon which branch of the tree they inhabit: Yeye, Laoye. Our daughter is Gugu, our younger son Shushu, both titles that denote which side of the family they come from. It's all codified in a way that, my son says, is very Chinese, but we discovered that the Swedes do it, too. A nice young Swedish woman filled me in one day at lunch: Mormor, Morfar, Farmor, Farfar. A Hindi student told me her maternal grandparents are Nani and Nana, her paternal ones Dadi and Dada.

Which brings us to what I think of as the nono's. These are the women who telegraph, at least privately to me, that they have mixed feelings about all this. The aging beauty who asked to be called Glamma. A socialite who told me she'd invented the name Tootsie. Some of them say they are not interested in surrogate mothering. "I'm going to be a grandmother the way my grandmother was, watching their mother chase them around," one woman told me. "I'm happy to be a grandmother, but I don't want to be a babysitter," another woman said. If you want to see a real food fight online, look at the women talking about the refusal of their mother, or their mother-in-law, to take care of the grandchildren on a regular basis. I know many women who have signed on for childcare a day or two a week, and are delighted to do so, but others say that, while they love their grandchildren, they spent years raising their own kids and don't want to revisit the experience at this point in their lives. It's too exhausting. It's too time-consuming. They're still working. They have other priorities.

But for many of the nono's, the issue is not time management but growing older. There is no question that whether you are forty or seventy, the simple fact of being a grandparent telegraphs aging. Whatever you may be, you are no longer the young one. We were once buffered by generations: the elders, the parents, the older cousins. In what seemed like record time, we have become the elders, standing at the prow of the ship, figureheads with nothing between us and the wild wind but a vista of open sea stretching to the sheer drop of the horizon. This is one of those feelings only reinforced by becoming a grandparent, and one reason becoming a grandparent freaks some people out.

Along with the nono's I also meet a fair number of what I'll call do-over grandmothers. For one reason or another they think they didn't get it quite right when they were raising their own children, and they believe they will be able to bring their best selves to the table, which is a luxury you have when you're a grandparent. You're rarely the one snatching them up from school after you've had a tough day at work and then facing an empty fridge and a full hamper as well as a querulous kid who forgot the homework assignment sheet and might be coming down with something. Grandparents usually get the best-case-scenario kid, and even when they don't, their time together has a sell-by date. The parents return. The grandchild leaves.

That scenario is not true for everyone. At the moment there are many more grandparents raising their grandchildren full time than in previous decades, or perhaps ever. Some of that is due to drug addiction and parents who are too addled or ill to care for their children themselves. Some is teenage pregnancy in an era when pregnant teenagers no longer feel compelled to give their children up for adoption or enter into early marriage. Many of these grandparents don't have formal custody; their grandchildren's father and mother may not want them now, but that doesn't mean they won't show up in a year or two, minds changed, kids reclaimed, hearts broken. The parenting grandparents are exhausted, too, and with better reason than most of us, although they also often describe themselves as exhilarated by the chance to raise children again and, given the insufficiencies of their own kids that led to this situation, to get it right this time.

It's interesting, the things age teaches you, not all of them about hip joints and slack skin. I can't imagine anyone ever thinks to herself, at twenty-five, Someday I will get to be a grandmother. None of us grew up thinking that playing Candy Land at age seventy was our birthright or even our end-game. But the years went by, and our nests grew empty. And while we had once hoped that our children would do better than we had in a variety of ways, we began to hope they would mimic us in one crucial role, that of parent.

But while there are more grandparents then ever before, there are also many people for whom the role seems either elusive or impossible. The fertility rate in the United States as well as in many other countries has plummeted in recent years. Couples conclude that it's expensive to have children. Women are wage earners with fulfilling jobs that they are loath to interrupt or to leave. And, let's be honest: for every story you've heard about the enormous satisfaction of being a parent, the amusing and endearing anecdotes, the vacation photos with beach tans and big grins, there are all the other stories. The kids with terrible emotional problems. The teenagers teetering on the verge of felony and mayhem. The young adults who happily blew through usurious college tuitions without finishing and without gratitude. The grown children who, for reasons odd and obscure, barely speak to their parents. It's just as easy to conclude that parenthood is a glass half empty as half full, never mind all full, and to decide that having children is not for you. Which means having grandchildren is not for your parents.

And then there are the grown children who are happily married, always in touch, terrific company available for anything from an elaborate home-cooked meal to takeout containers of pad thai, the kind of people you'd dreamed they would become when they were throwing a tantrum in the grocery aisle or slamming the bedroom door during early adolescence. The bridesmaids and ushers at their weddings, their friends from college and high school: you've seen one birth announcement and one shower invitation after another. Maybe at one of those showers someone's mother is even pushy enough to say, what are you waiting for? And then your son tells you solemnly, his wife in tears, or your daughter sobs into your shoulder, her husband patting her back gently, that they've been trying for years, doctors, tests, shots, that for some reason, known or unknown, it is not happening for them, this thing that seems so easy for everyone else.

The point is that just as some younger people have had to venture into a brave new world in which children are not a given, perhaps not even a goal, their mothers and fathers have been dragged along for the ride.

The sons and daughters who decide against having children can't help but make some of their mothers and fathers feel as though it's an indictment of their own childhoods and upbringings. The ones who are foreclosed by biology can't help but make some of their mothers and fathers feel as though they've sustained a great bereavement.

Becoming a parent is frequently under your control, although those people undergoing in vitro fertilization could argue differently. Becoming a grandparent is totally under the control of others, as any would-be nana who has hinted, cajoled, begged, and passed along endless photographs of other people's grandchildren can attest. ("Look at how cute! Twins! And she was two years behind you in high school!") Understanding this is the first step to understanding that what sort of grandparent you will be permitted to be is also under their control. Everyday nana. Occasional nana. Seldom. Never.

Once again we are reminded that there are no guarantees, that we make plans and God says Ha, that we work with the family hand we are dealt. When Arthur was introduced in a plastic bin and striped swaddle within the walls of Mount Sinai Hospital, he had four grandparents in the room, two from each side, a full conventional complement. This is apparently a bit of a throwback; one young woman described the somewhat uneasy gathering of her father, his second wife, her mother, her father-in-law, her mother-in-law, and her mother-in-law's boyfriend. At least her father-in-law didn't bring his new wife along. One thorny nomenclature issue today is what to call the stepgrandmothers. Families today seem more complicated than they once were, which means grandparenting is, too.

Joan Didion once wrote that we tell ourselves stories in order to live, but I think we tell ourselves family stories in order to exist, to feel really real. This seems especially true nowadays. The independence and individuality of modern life need to be leavened with an understanding of our place at the table, and often today people find that through genealogy, which is undergoing an enormous boom. In decades past it was a bit beside the point: when I was growing up, almost every member not only of my father's family but of his father's family lived within an easy car ride. I was rooted firmly within the branches of my family tree, even though I often found it a tangle. But people are more mobile now, and spread around the country and the world, and as families have grown ever smaller the thirst to become part of something larger has grown, too.

I suppose that's what some of my friends yearn for, knowing that they will never be grandparents. Reading history, looking around us, we have gotten accustomed to the feeling that family is eternal, spooling into the future without end. I have that feeling very powerfully now in a way I did not before my grandson was born. This is my afterlife. The children, the grandchildren: as long as they have stories to tell, I live. If the stories are good enough, I live for a long long time. Arthur Krovatin: life everlasting.

Maybe that's why I am happily a nana and not in the least a nono, why I never once have said, "I feel too young to be a grandmother." I don't care that much about getting older, but I don't want to be forgotten, because to be remembered is to live and to be loved. What remains when the synapses have begun to die, when we ourselves are gone? Jorge Luis Borges said, "When writers die they become books, which is, after all, not too bad an incarnation." When mothers die they leave children, and when nanas die they leave grandchildren and perhaps a trace memory of being coddled, kissed, attended to, and loved, of being chased across the lawn or rocked in the middle of the night or taken seriously. In Nanaville there is always in the back of my mind the understanding that I am building a memory out of spare parts and that, someday, that memory will be all that's left of me.

# LUCK OF THE DRAW

My kids are a pretty tough crowd. "What do you bring to the party?" might be one of their mottoes. So when the younger two came home from visiting their brother in China united in their appreciation for the woman who was his girlfriend, I was pretty impressed. There was no carping, and as someone who has herself been carped about plenty by this group, I was somewhat envious. But not for long.

On paper the woman who would become our first daughter-in-law sounded like a bit of a crapshoot: an only child, while my three constituted a spontaneous flash mob; the daughter of a Communist atheist country, whose boyfriend's family had deep Catholic roots. One of the first times we were together was at the San Gennaro festival in Little Italy. She definitely got the point of the calzone and the zeppole—if she hadn't, that would have been a deal breaker, because fried dough, come on—but she was perplexed by San Gennaro himself. It wasn't just him; it was the whole concept of saints, a concept that is as natural to me as breath. Show me a stained-glass window with a rendering of a guy crucified on an X-shaped cross or a nun with her arms full of roses and I can tell you who they are without even thinking hard. (St. Andrew and Thérèse of Lisieux, for the record.) But when I started to describe the canonization process, the miracles and the relics, the whole deal from the ground up, I realized it sounded quite peculiar.

The woman who married our eldest child is nothing if not sane, and smart, and wonderful to be with, even as she's looking quizzical while you describe the transubstantiation. A thousand times since she showed up, at the dining room table or at the shopping outlets, working out with her or watching her crack up with my daughter and younger son, I've thought to myself: boy, did we luck out. Soon after she was married, someone asked her if she had any siblings. "Now I do," she said.

See what I mean?

This has become ever clearer as she has morphed from girlfriend to wife to mother of our grandchild. The addition of a baby into the mix throws the relationship between you and your daughter-in-law into high relief, the good times and the bad, the joy and the sorrow, as our daughter-in-law once heard our friend the judge say as she stood in a white dress holding a bouquet in a field full of interested parties. Over the years I have discovered through observation that there are many kinds of daughters-in-law:

- The ones who are really, really nice when they are dating your son and then, once married, not so much.
- The ones who are really, really nice when they are married to your son and then, once they have children, not so much.

- The ones who believe in the one-woman man and think they should be that one woman, which means eliminating the mother.
- The ones who are very, very close to their own family, which means yours is secondary, if not fungible.
- The ones waiting patiently for you to make what they consider a critical mistake, which will lead your son to say sorrowfully, "She's not really that comfortable leaving the kids with you," as though you are the kind of person who lets toddlers play with matches and scissors, as though you are not the person who raised a boy into the man who is now selling you out.
- The great ones, who more or less roll with everything.

Since their baby was born, it has become very clear: somehow, luck of the draw, when my son met a woman in an expat bar in Beijing, we wound up with one of those last. And I know it. And I thank God for it, did when I was just the mother-in-law, double-do as the nana. Because when your son becomes a father, so much that follows depends on how your daughter-in-law feels about you. I saw an article once about advice to the mother of the groom. The headline read: WEAR BEIGE AND KEEP YOUR MOUTH SHUT.

I look bad in beige.

Times have changed on the woman/man, wife/husband, mother/father continuum. Perhaps it was best summed up for me the day I was running in the park and came upon what I can only describe as a pack of bros. You know the type: khaki shorts, pink polo shirts, conservative haircuts. Brooks Brothers, not Birkenstocks. And yet each of them had one notable accessory: a high-end stroller. Well, a high-end stroller with a baby in it. One of them had stopped because the binky had fallen out of the baby's mouth and all hell had broken loose. I have to say, he wiped that pacifier off very assiduously while the other two watched and waited. Then they moved on, a dad phalanx.

Now, my children's father in fact did

push a stroller from time to time, but rarely on a weekday and certainly not with a bunch of buddies. Just like he did school drop-off from time to time but not virtually every day, the way our son does. I don't know that my father ever actually laid hands on a stroller, although he did teach me to fish and to tell the difference between an alto and a tenor sax in a jazz recording. I can promise you that neither of my grandfathers ever pushed a stroller. Fatherhood has moved along a continuum during our lifetimes so that the hands-on dad who wears the baby carrier and does the school run has become a commonplace.

But one thing that seems to have changed little is that many women still control the agenda of a hetero family. Research has even shown that grandparents are more likely to see the children of their daughters than the children of their sons because of these sex-specific social arrangements. And what that all means is that if your daughter-in-law likes you, you're in luck. And if not, not. This is why I said for years that the most important decision your sons would make was whom they married. This is why I heaved a sigh of relief when both chose women whom we liked.

I have heard all the alternative stories, so I knew. Of the DIL who asked, "What are you two planning for Thanksgiving?" after mentioning that she was cooking for her entire side of the family. Of the one who always cancels coming for Sunday dinner on Friday afternoon. Of the ones who live in other places and never bring the kids for a visit, and the ones who live in the same place you do and, somehow, ditto. It's hard work, navigating the vagaries of a sort-of daughter not your own. I suppose the good news is that eventually grandchildren make their own decisions about who to cleave to, and the nana who may be an occasional visitor from the big city for a toddler becomes the nana whose big-city apartment is the destination of choice for a teenager.

In the meantime, only patience is possible, although it would be lovely if it worked both ways. One young woman said to me of the grandmother of her children, "She buys them the kind of clothes that kids don't really wear." I happen to know her mother-in-law, who said, "I never see the kids in the outfits I buy them." And in those two sentences was an entire universe of disconnect that I assumed would have been worked out had the two been mother and daughter instead of in-laws. Although perhaps not.

Naturally I've heard the son-in-law stories, too, of the ones who have laid down the law about grandparent visits, or the ones who want grandparents to pay for something, access to the grandchild contingent on checkbook. But more of those stories end with a daughter bringing the kids over on Sunday afternoons on her own, trailing excuses about how busy her husband is, or how he has a standing golf date with people from work, or how he has a touch of bubonic plague but almost certainly will show up next time. In our more egalitarian age, the equivalent would be the son who brings the kids to see you on Sundays even if his wife prefers to watch TV and mull over some passing remark you made at her bridal shower that seems rather anodyne but which she will never, ever forget. Maybe I just hear fewer of those stories. And, to be fair, I hear fewer stories about how the SIL doesn't pitch in enough and more about how the DIL has ridiculous dietary rules for the kids and never writes thank-you notes. Apparently thank-you emails don't count.

Having been a DIL myself, I was ready to give my first DIL as much latitude as my mother-in-law gave me—and believe me, as a DIL I was a lot. But that's been unnecessary. Diligent, accomplished, she has done her best at virtually everything she's touched. But, as with my son, her husband, I'm not sure that on paper I would have figured her for the excellent mother she's turned out to be. She told me once that she was out with her girlfriends and said in passing that she didn't think she'd be the hard guy, the enforcer, a tiger mother, and that they all goggled at her and then busted up laughing. She is in fact that person but with that sense of love and fun that leavens it and turns it into really good parenting. "Where are you, my angel?" I hear her call in a singsong voice across the lawn to her son, and my heart lifts. If she were my mother, I would feel loved.

From the beginning she has been open to our hands-on involvement in the life of her son, and we have been open to providing it if we're able. Sometimes I ask, and she has other plans. Sometimes she asks, and I do. But there's no drama to any of this. If she says no I don't read it as an insult, because when I say no she doesn't read it that way. When her baby was only a few weeks old, she and our son came out to live at our house in the country for the summer, so that I got to observe and participate in the earliest weeks of our grandson's life. "You are so lucky!" all my friends told me, and I agreed, but it was really only afterward that I realized how remarkable that was and how much confidence a person would have to have to do it. You're never more unsure of yourself than when your first child is still nearly fetal, even if you're from a big family and have diapered a few babies when you weren't much more than an overgrown baby yourself. I'm not sure I would have been comfortable sharing the earliest days of my first child's life with my mother-in-law, a woman who had raised six sons. She might not have been judgmental, but I suspect I would have been judging myself harshly, and mightily inclined to make myself feel better by assigning that judgment to her. Thus do the Sunday afternoon schisms begin. The baby cries. Your mother-in-law looks up. She is thinking, I wonder why he's crying. Or maybe she's just thinking, I don't think that soup I had for lunch is agreeing with me, or, I wonder when those shoes I ordered online will arrive. But you are the DIL, so when she looks up you might assume that she is thinking, That girl doesn't really know how to take care of a baby.

"Can I take him?" the nana might ask, and you will say, "No, no, I've got him. It's fine."

Luck of the draw: one afternoon we are walking around the pond. It's late in the day, drawing in on what someone described many years ago as the arsenic hours, that time when small children unravel like an old sweater. Arthur is unraveling for sure. I read somewhere that when interrogators are holding suspected terrorists, they pipe heavy-metal music continuously, loudly, into their cells, which they think makes people more likely to break and talk. Me, all you would have to do is play a crying infant continuously and I would cop to almost anything, from shoplifting to serial killing.

I draw up next to my daughter-in-law as the keening continues and hold out my arms. Without hesitating a moment she hands her son, my grandson, to me. "Give it a shot," she says.

## SMALL MOMENTS

Family dinner, Easter Sunday. Everyone is hungry, because the older ones have outgrown the Easter basket, or at least outgrown trying to eat an entire hollow chocolate bunny at one sitting, and the youngest among us has not yet been given free rein. He is in his booster seat, and he is not eating much. One of the great things about being a nana is seeing things from the perspective of a small person: soda bubbles go right up your nose, bugs crawling across the pavement are mesmerizing. One day, walking down the long driveway, Arthur discovered his shadow. Boy, that was something. Move leg; shadow moves leg. Wiggle fingers; shadow wiggles fingers. Walk and it walks to one side of you. Eventually it got tedious, but before the tedium was the surprised recognition that I hadn't thought about my shadow in decades, that down to its essence it was a pretty wild concept. Nana walks. Nana's shadow walks. Wow. What a time we had.

At Easter dinner I realize that ham has a weird texture. Think about it: like a salty pencil eraser. We are all digging in and Arthur is chewing, then taking the chewed food out of his mouth with a bemused grimace, looking at it, and finally putting it on the tray of his booster seat. I bought and made the ham, but suddenly the ham feels weird in my mouth. Still I chew and swallow, because the nana has to set a good example, which is why I am still trying to swear less, damn it. First time a dog eases a bagel from this child's hand and the child lets out a dirty word, I am going to be in big trouble with everyone. He already said "Oh my God" one day. I would say he picked it up elsewhere, but he sounded just like me.

But Nana is empathizing, too, so that when Arthur takes one last piece of ham from his mouth and says, "All done," I am ready to let him get down from his booster seat.

Not his mother, who insists he remain until dinner is over. Which reminds me that in this government, in terms of the line of succession, I am either the speaker of the house or the president pro tem of the Senate but definitely not the president or the vice president. I do not have the right to sign off or veto.

The problem with empathy for the children in your life is that there is a fine line between identification and indulgence. Conventional wisdom has it that indulgence is the privilege of grandparents, and I suppose there's some truth to that in terms of serving dessert even if there wasn't much eaten at dinner. But parents aren't that wild about grandparents who indulge too much, because it sometimes makes them feel one-upped or disrespected. And respecting the parents, as you can tell, is the linchpin of success in Nanaville.

And sometimes empathy can lead you astray. It's all well and good to say that you hated summer book reports, too, but the summer book reports still need to be done. I was conspicuously empathetic when all three of my children sucked their thumbs, since I was what you might call an accomplished thumb-sucker, up to an age that I would mention except that it's much too embarrassing. But I found myself blowing off the orthodontist over and over again, until one day I realized that my children were not me—which is, of course, the biggest moment in your progression as a parent, and for some people never arrives—and that they needed to stop thumb-sucking. I will add that I did not resort to the usual noxious substance on their thumbs, since that was tried on me many times and I just sucked the stuff off. In one case bribery was involved, and that's how my daughter got her ears pierced.

So Arthur stayed at the table until the rest of us were done with our ham. He didn't make a fuss. I didn't act precipitously. Eventually he said, "Excused please, Mama," and was allowed to slide out of his seat and down to the floor.

Lessons learned:

- "No" does not mean "I don't love you." It just means no.

- Manners can be taught early.

- Hang back. I cannot repeat this one often enough. Hang back.

# THIS IS WHAT THE FUTURE
# LOOKS LIKE

After Arthur was born, the pediatrician flipped him onto his stomach so his parents could consider his buttocks. Spreading across them was an irregular area almost as big as my hand, which was the color of a lowering sky before a storm. It was something called a Mongolian blue spot, a congenital birthmark almost universal in Asian babies. One reincarnation story has it that some souls were unwilling to be reborn and that they had to be forced from the womb, leaving what looks like an enormous bruise on the back end. I'd never heard of a Mongolian blue spot, and neither have many other people, which is why the doctor was explaining it to Arthur's parents, because in communities unfamiliar with Asian babies it is sometimes mistaken for a sign of abuse.

This is what our country looks like now. This is what the world looks like. The child who has one parent who is black and another who is white. The child who has one parent who is Latino and another who is Swedish and who ricochets among languages, sometimes mixing them up in a single sentence. The year our first grandchild was born, one in seven new babies in America was multiracial or multiethnic, almost triple the number in the year my eldest child, his father, was born. And this in a country that when I was young banned interracial marriage in many states.

The arc of progress bends toward grandchildren that are like us and yet not. When I was a child the lines between countries and cultures were wider, barely semipermeable. I knew one Asian girl, who had been adopted from Korea when she was a baby; there always hung about her some persistent sense of do-gooding on the part of her parents, as well as an aura of difference so glaring that it was incandescent. The number of times neighborhood kids thought it was hilarious to pull their eyes tight at the corners to mock her was infinite. Where I grew up, a mixed marriage was between a Catholic and a Lutheran who had, naturally, converted.

And then there was my family. All my father's brothers had married within the Irish clan: Reilly, Kelly, the kind of women who knew how to serve corned beef and cabbage and wore a lot of navy blue. My father married a woman whose surname was Pantano, who could bang out a pizza rustica without thinking twice and looked slamming in a red dress. It sounds so silly to say it now, when my parents' union would be so unremarkable, but it was a bit of a deal, like the Sharks (Puerto Rican) and the Jets (Anglo) of **West Side Story**. Which is, of course, based on **Romeo and Juliet**, and the Montagues and Capulets. Everything changes and nothing changes. My sister reports that the high school students she teaches still exist in silos: the Latino students beef with the Samoans; the black students bully the Chinese, who are seen as having some special status. The capacity of human beings to create an exclusionary society knows no bounds, even when those bounds are stretched or seem to be broken. Until the moment when you are handed a baby, who breaches them entirely.

The world has changed since my grandparents presided over a welter of purely white grandchildren. As I grew to adulthood there was more travel, more intermingling of ethnicity and race. More people went to college, where they often met people who were substantially different than they were in some essential way. I have two daughters-in-law. One is biracial. One is Chinese. Well, kind of. When people ask Lynn Feng where she is from, she likes to mess with them a little bit and say, "Lawrence, Kansas." Which is actually where she spent her formative years.

She's gotten a lot of this, and I've appreciated it more since Arthur was born. Twice it happened when I had him in the baby sling, both times when I was standing in line, once for produce, once for a snowsuit. The first time it was a woman: "Where did you get him?" she asked, and I was speechless. The second time, I'm not sure why, my inner smart-ass came out to play. "Where did you get him?" said the man in Baby Gap. "Whole Foods," I replied, inexplicably.

This is obviously because my grandson is Chinese and I am not. But he is also Irish, Italian, Slovenian—maybe some German or Austrian, but Pop is less sure of his bloodlines than I am, and his may be more polyglot than my own or than he knows. I come from Irish who married other Irish for many generations and Italians who did the same, until one from each side of the street became a crack jitterbugger and met, danced, dated, fell in love, married, and had me. Some of those involved were not pleased. My father lived with his in-laws for the first year of my life, and he learned to recognize an Italian sentence that, translated, means, "He eats like a bird."

But our eldest grandson's maternal side is pure and unadulterated Chinese. I find this all miraculous, and strange, and I warrant his maternal grandparents do, too.

Shengli Feng and Yaping Yu went from Beijing, where they were born, to the countryside, where they were sent for something termed "reeducation," and then to the United States, where they did graduate work and became professors and raised their daughter in a university town. Across the world, Gerry Krovatin and Anna Quindlen grew up as Catholic children steeped in the need for missionaries to convert the so-called Red Chinese, realized in college that this was errant nonsense, learned to use chopsticks at Chinese restaurants in places that served the kind of food Americans think of as Chinese and Chinese people think of as nothing they've ever eaten at home.

In the best sense their children expanded their existence, and their minds. They introduced them to plays they would not have seen had their children not been acting in them. They made them watch movies they might have skipped, read books they could have passed over. When their eldest child went to live in Beijing after college, they toured the Forbidden City, hiked the Great Wall, ate in restaurants where their son ordered and the waitress clapped her hands and said, delighted, "He speaks Chinese!" Thank God he does, because his in-laws certainly do, and always have.

But he and his brother have also introduced us to something else we hadn't really experienced firsthand in a particular sort of way, and that's stereotype and perhaps, as time goes by, the rawest sort of prejudice. A sophisticated acquaintance said to me of my first grandchild, "Well, at least you won't have to worry about his math scores." Now, there are surely worse things than being told that a kid is bound to be sitting in advanced calculus someday, and maybe this will turn out to be true. (His father certainly did, and he wasn't Chinese!) But even so-called positive stereotypes are stereotypes; what's called the Model Minority Myth has been dogging Asians for decades. As for my second son, whose future children will have three Caucasian grandparents and one who is a black woman from Belize, he's already thinking about hard conversations he might have with his future sons about interactions with the police. His wife describes occasions on which passersby assumed that her mother was the nanny—of her own children. I imagine this to be a particular kind of humiliation that provokes a particular sort of anger, at the same time remembering that I have no real clue about the various injuries that come with being a person of color in a country that, at least for now, has white as its default setting. It's not exactly the same, but perhaps because my mother was such a mild-mannered woman, I can recall vividly the times she talked about being insulted as an Italian girl. She spat the words: "Dago." "Wop." "Guinea." She said them as though they were profanities.

But because of my own background I also keep thinking about the positive attributes of swimming in various gene pools, and not simply the advantage identified by the genetic counselor Arthur's parents saw when he was still in utero, who said, "There is no genetic overlap between the two of you." Historians can attest to the downside of single-strand bloodlines; Queen Victoria married her grandchildren off selectively to keep the royal family tree pure and in the process created one in which hemophilia ran rampant.

I felt a bit of whiplash involved in being Irish/Italian, an either/or, even in what today seems like a very minimal way. And I know some people insist that racial or ethnic intermingling has left them feeling as though they were moored nowhere, neither this nor that. But I feel as though it built in me a vague sense that I was an everything, that there was no template to which to hew, as there would have been had I been purely one or the other. I feel that all the time with Arthur. So much of it now focuses on his appearance. There's a celebrity magazine trick that they do with computers that I think of when I look at him, where they take two photos and morph them into one face to show what the child of Pop Star and Franchise Actor might look like.

"He looks so much like you!" someone will say to his (Caucasian) father. "He looks just like you!" someone else will say to his (Asian) mother. And at various times both of those things have been accurate, and then he turns aside, makes a face, and he is both, and neither. He is his own self.

That's one of the challenges for many parents, and the source of liberation for many grandparents. Having no expectations is extraordinarily difficult. I tried so hard not to make assumptions about our own children, assumptions about what they would do and be and think and want. And I made those assumptions all the time, unconsciously and reflexively, based not on their needs but on mine. I particularly did that with my eldest child, not only because I am an eldest child myself but because, let's face it, he was the person I practiced on before I got the hang of motherhood. I was somewhat better with the other two, but I would probably give myself a B at best, and that's grading on a curve, next to some parents I knew who never let their children, for example, consider any college but their own alma mater.

But—and I may eat these words some-day, I know—I feel as though I got a lot of that out of my system and that I really do look at Arthur and wonder what he will become, without spending much time wishing he would choose a given path. He isn't a bit like his father when he was his age, and I don't know precisely what his mother was like as a child, but I keep thinking that being a grandparent is the opportunity to put much of that aside and simply sit and wait and see. And the fact that he is made up of such disparate component parts helps make this possible. "He isn't like anyone else in the family," a woman said to me one day about her grandson, who can delve into the soul of the computer as though he were a cyber exorcist and who has tried but failed to explain to his granny, as he calls her, what exactly he is doing.

Then she added, "Isn't that wonderful?" And all I could do was nod enthusiastically. It surely is.

# SMALL MOMENTS

The cupboard is full of teacups, the fine-skinned porcelain sort that, clinked together, make the high sound of a tiny bell. There are saucers, too, part of an ensemble that, when I was a kid, was trotted out for something called luncheon. For many years this was what you would ask for as a wedding gift, these sorts of dishes. But they got used seldom, and I asked instead for a stewpot and a food processor. These teacups, these saucers, are cherished because they once belonged to my mother, the woman who would be my children's nana if she were still alive.

They are always dusty. I never use them.

I am a mug person. I love coffee, and I like a lot of it, and I don't want to fool with refills. When I go to a coffee bar, it's the biggest size I order, whatever they call it. It's my one problem with Italy, even though I'm half Italian and think the sentence "How was your vacation in Italy?" is never anything but a rhetorical question. But still. Love your people, your food, your art, your leather goods, but those tiny espresso cups. Please.

I've lived a life in mugs, one after another. There were handmade pottery mugs from craft fairs and big café au lait terrines from a French bistro selling off its stock. There was one that had the First Amendment on it—forgive me, I'm a recovering reporter—and another with the text of the Equal Rights Amendment, which was incredibly controversial because it said women should be treated like people.

There was the one that said BECAUSE I'M THE MOM, THAT'S WHY. There was the one that said COOL MOM, which was kind of a lie and didn't last long. If memory serves, and it so rarely does, there was a succession of Mom mugs.

But the one to which I became most attached was one given to me by my son Christopher, who is also responsible for all my nun paraphernalia, including the giant rubber doll on one desk and the vintage nun doll in a removable habit on the other. (And, no, the removable habit has never been removed.) A gloss on the title of my novel published that year, that mug read RISE AND WHINE. Over time the yellow glaze chipped. A divot at one corner meant I had to be careful where I put my mouth. The handle broke off, which is why God invented Krazy Glue. (God invented coffee, too. Duh.)

And then one day I was making a histrionic gesture with my arm, and I swept that mug off the table and onto the floor, where it broke into pieces so tiny that I was pulling them from my bare feet for days.

"Chris, I know what you can get me for Christmas," I said.

Apparently he searched and searched for

an identical mug, to no avail. The fashions in novelty coffee mugs morph over the years, along with mores and slang. There are now, for example, any number of mugs with the kind of profanity that would have made my grandmother's luncheon crowd gasp as they held their porcelain. COOL MOM seems to have given way to EVERY GREAT MOM SAYS THE F-WORD.

But luckily the timing was perfect for Chris to go in a different direction. And so on Christmas morning I unwrapped a new mug, big enough to hold a whole boatload of demitasse espresso. It's brightly colored, with semi-psychedelic flowers, and it says, IT'S GRAND TO BE NANA. It's pretty unbreakable, too, that hard-glazed pottery that is the antithesis of the elegant thin-skinned teacups for company. I feel as though the rest of my days will be like this, living amid things that can't get broken, mangled, or dirtied up, so that the grandkids will have free rein in my house. After all, no décor, no matter how beautiful, is an adequate trade-off for playing fort under a quilt draped over a table on a rainy day.

It's grand to be Nana.
I'll drink to that.
Lessons learned:

- One mug shatters and another one appears.

- There is never enough coffee.

- A lucky woman gets to trade her MOM mugs in for a NANA mug.

# THIS IS HOW IT
# BEGINS, AGAIN

We searched for the signs. We tried to keep our counsel. Our daughter-in-law passed on wine with dinner. She didn't have coffee in the morning. In the car to the country she turned, her father-in-law noted, undeniably green.

"Lynn's pregnant," our son said on a video call with his sister, as his son sat in his high chair and everyone gathered around the table.

Arthur looked terribly concerned as his aunt started to cry. "Gugu is happy, honey," I said. "Really, she's so happy."

"I'm really happy," Maria sobbed.

And so it begins again. Or maybe it began

months ago, when they looked at one another and thought, it's time, or even a year ago, when they watched their son try to climb the ladder to the slide and thought, it would be good for him to have a brother or sister to play with. Come to think of it, it probably began for our son many many years ago. His brother and his sister have been a pivotal part of his life forever; because he and his brother are so close in age, he has no memory of a time when he was the only child. His wife knows that. And despite a lifetime as an only child, her newly minted siblings are an important part of her life, as well.

They will be different this time. They don't know that yet, but I do. It turns out your heart is a balloon: it expands effortlessly. Your hands, not so much. It ought to be that two is one plus one, but two children is actually one plus one plus a hundred, or a thousand, or something, depending on the day. With the first one you nurse a baby, the silence deep and sweet, the smell of new hair and skin perfuming the air. With the second you nurse a baby while the elder child takes mustard from the fridge and paints the tile floor with it.

That actually once happened. And our elder child was on the easy end of the toddler number line. Still. The first year after our second child arrived is a complete blur to me in many ways. I wanted to have a third child right away—what can I say, my hormones were raging—and my husband said evenly, "You've been in a bad mood for six months. Maybe we should wait a little while." Which, while maddening—like I said, hormones—happened to be accurate. The space between the second and third was somewhat larger than the space between the first and second. "Three?" people said. Three. It was all pretty wild, going from a man-to-man to a zone defense.

I wouldn't change a thing. About any of it.

I will be different this time, too. When I first tried my hand at stand-up paddleboarding, one of the women I was with pulled up next to me and began to fill me in on what I needed to change as I paddled, how my arms were at the wrong angle, how far I needed to push into the water, and precisely how to sweep back. I stared straight ahead and, without looking at her, I said between gritted teeth, "All I can do right now is try to stand up on this thing."

It's such an apt metaphor for almost everything I've ever done in my life. I know how to use my paddle now, how to use it to move swiftly through the water, how to turn my board. But the beginning of everything is just trying to nail the most primitive part, to tame the lizard brain that says you can't, don't try, you'll fall.

In the beginning of my life in Nanaville, I was just trying to stay standing. I made up so much of the mothering thing as I went, and even more of the grandmothering thing. If it's not clear enough here, mistakes were made. But they were made out of haste and ignorance, lack of thought but never lack of love.

I remember setting up a nursery for Arthur at our house for grandchild visits. I was so proud of how pretty it looked. The patterned crib sheets, the harmonizing bumpers with those little bows to tie them to the crib slats, a velvety quilt, a pillow Nana had needlepointed of the three bears, a fluffy stuffed lamb: the whole deal was shelter magazine, if I do say so myself.

Out went the bumpers, the quilt, the pillow, and the stuffed animal, because the current thinking is that for infants to sleep safely there should be nothing in the crib but . . . nothing. Well, the sheet stayed. The pillow went on the rocking chair. I had the obligatory moment of thinking, but not saying, that it looked so bare and sad.

But I realized that the only thing in the crib that mattered at all was the baby.

No bumpers for the second. I'm broken in now. That's the job of the first, to teach you the ropes. That's the trade-off: they get the kind of attention and focus that only a single child gets, that gathering of adults that can't help but look like an audience. And in return they must become unwitting tutors: the baby who teaches you how to put on a onesie without bending him like a Gumby doll, the toddler who teaches you how to ignore opposition instead of engaging with it:

But you love chicken!

You're going to have a bath whether you want it or not!

Don't you dare get out of that crib!

This child will be different, too, an entirely distinct person. To begin with, she will be female, a sunnu, a granddaughter, not a sunzi, a grandson. Another new word to learn in Mandarin. Wo ai ni, sunnu. We had no idea of the sex of our own children until we met them in the birthing room, but because of the many diagnostic tests now available, this generation usually knows what is coming, at least in this regard. When she found out, our daughter-in-law immediately began to worry about how she could make certain she wasn't gifted a lot of pink. Lynn is not a pink person. Neither am I. But her daughter may be. This is what we learn, that we imagine them and then they are different than our imaginings. I keep realizing that how I imagined Arthur didn't come close to the thrill of the reality.

This new baby's father, my son, said what perhaps every good man under the sun has said, that he is concerned because he was once a boy, he understands what it means to be a boy becoming a man, but he doesn't know what it's like to be a girl. Luckily, his wife was once a girl, and so was I, and so was his sister. Even more luckily, he has always been so comfortable with women, especially strong women. So many of his friends have been female. He will be fine. He will be better than fine.

I suppose the gender difference will help at least a little bit with our natural inclination to think of the second child as a sequel, when in fact the second child is a completely unique story. I will try to help make sure that number two never feels like number two, and the same with three or four if and when they arrive. But I will also try to make sure that number one never feels supplanted. Pop and Nana, eldest children both, clearly remember being pushed down the greasy pole of attention and up the steep stairs of responsibility. That will be a new part of our job, making sure Arthur understands that nothing has changed. Which, of course, isn't true. Everything changes, including Nanaville.

I am different now, because I know what I am and what I am not. I am not Santa. Someone told me not long ago that there is a new phenomenon abroad in the land, the grandmother baby shower. The notion is that, since your grandchildren will be spending a lot of time at your house, your friends can gift you those things that you may need to care for and entertain them. The problem is that it also suggests that this is all about you. And it's not all about you. Grandmothers are important, but they must calibrate their places carefully, and under a bouquet of balloons surrounded by boxes of baby gear is not, as far as I'm concerned, my rightful place.

I know my rightful place now.

Science tells me, however, happily, that I am even more essential than the first time out. One anthropologist studied an African tribe of hunter-gatherers and found that the hunters, the men, were rarely successful. The tribe would have starved if it had relied on them alone, or even primarily, for sustenance. It was the gatherers, the women, who provided most of the food, by working the earth. A mother who dug successfully for tubers had a healthy child. But with a second child, the amount of food a grandmother gathered became important, as well. In other words, as families grow, grandparents become even more critical to their well-being. Nana may be called on to wrangle one while the other has alone time with the parents, or to wrangle two so the parents have alone time with one another, alone time that I know from experience they will mainly spend talking about the children. Out of sight but never out of mind.

Families are crucibles of so much that shapes and steers and, sometimes, damages us. It's odd when you look at animals and realize that once the puppies have been weaned and have grown, their mother doesn't seem to recognize any trace relationship with them. That's not true of humans, for good and for ill. Like those plastic monkeys I bought for the baby shower, because Arthur was going to be born in the Chinese year of the monkey, we link together in a chain that is undeniable even if we try to break it. I had one family, and it got bigger and bigger, and then it began to get smaller for a while, and then it grew again. We were the children, then the parents, now the grandparents.

It will all be different this time, and in some ways it will all be the same. This baby's birth date is in the Chinese year of the pig. Energetic, realistic, enthusiastic, a social butterfly, according to the zodiac site, as opposed to the older brother's monkey sign, intelligent, logical, hot-tempered, a leader. The alchemy is yet uncertain, but alchemy there will be, as there always is. In the years to come, we may hear this again and again, and it will be different each and every time, but it will always be thrilling: we are having a baby.

# SMALL MOMENTS (IMAGINED)

I am sitting in one of the rockers on the front porch, trying to decide whether to stay or go. It's raining slightly, but it will soon stop and when it does I will continue talking to myself about this—not aloud, mind you, I try not to do it aloud—as I walk around the pond. How many times have I walked around this pond, rocked in these chairs? Too many to count. It is all the same as ever, but I am different. My knees ache a bit. My hips, too. It all makes sense since I am over eighty now, an age I never imagined when I was in my teens and twenties. It seemed like another country, getting old, when I was that age. The future seemed very far away. Now it seems very close and very narrow, the darker swath of sand on the pale beach where the water laps.

My grandchildren are that age now, and they have sent a message that they would like to come for the weekend with some friends. So I am trying to decide whether I should stay or go. They have been just like their parents in their feelings about this place. When they were little they searched for frogs in the frog pond, stalked snakes in the old stump, screamed as the dogs killed groundhogs, slept the drugged sleep of the exhausted child in their twin beds. When the fantail goldfish in the frog pond and the grass carp in the big pond died, I replaced them, hoping they would not notice, the same way I had once swapped out the old version of my eldest's ragged comfort object for a new one. (They noticed, all of them.) Sometimes in summer they stayed here for weeks at a time. Those were some of the most exhausting, and happiest, days of my life.

But then they reached middle school

and their interest waned. It was so booooor-
ring here. There was noooooothing to do.
Their parents were annoyed, but I had seen
it all before. There were years when our
children were in high school when we came
here only one weekend a month. They had
a choice: Saturday night in the city, or sitting in these old rockers looking out at the
lawn and the lightning bugs. At sixteen
that was no choice at all. Some parents told
us that we should just leave them alone in
town while we came out here, but we
thought that unwise. Actually, we thought
that borderline criminal.

And then, slowly, they circled back,
brought friends from college, spent a few
days here before going back to school. The
older they got, the more they gravitated to
this old house. It is happening again.
Everything happens again, over and over.
Life is a continuous loop. Until one day
it's not.

The rain has stopped.

They will bring bags full of groceries
and beer. They will bring books and bathing suits. Some of them will hike up the

mountain and see evidence of bear but not the bear itself. Some of them will lie by the pool and forget to reapply sunscreen and ask for aloe later. They will leave towels on the floor, some of them, and forget to strip the beds, and put something in the fridge that should be in the freezer, leaving me to track down a funny smell midweek. Depending on the friends, there may be an undercurrent of intrigue, or animus, or sexual tension. I will be more aware of this than any of them imagine. They think when you are old your senses dull, when they only sharpen.

I could go and spend the weekend in the city while they are here. Give them their privacy. Get out of their hair. They might be more likely to appreciate us at a distance: Oh, our grandparents, they're great. Yeah, we see them all the time.

That's not precisely true. They are all busy, busy in the way I was when I was their age. Me, not so much. But I feel lucky. They respond to my messages, stop by when they can. One of the differences between grandchildren and grandparents is that grandchildren think they have all the time in the world, and grandparents only wish they had.

I love them so, but it is an undemanding love. Through them I found myself capable of that.

Maybe I will stay; I will make myself scarce but soak up that feeling of being part of something so much larger than myself. In sixth grade one of them made a family tree, as so many sixth-graders have before, and there I was, below the trunk, right at the roots. If I live another decade or so, I might be a great-grandmother, the tree growing, expanding, flowering. That would be something, wouldn't it? That would really be something. If I were a great-grandmother, I wonder what I would call myself. I will have to think.

# ABOUT THE AUTHOR

ANNA QUINDLEN is a novelist and journalist whose work has appeared on fiction, nonfiction, and self-help bestseller lists. She is the author of nine novels: **Object Lessons, One True Thing, Black and Blue, Blessings, Rise and Shine, Every Last One, Still Life with Bread Crumbs, Miller's Valley**, and **Alternate Side**. Her memoir **Lots of Candles, Plenty of Cake**, published in 2012, was a **#1 New York Times** bestseller. Her book **A Short Guide to a Happy Life** has sold more than a million copies. While a columnist at **The New York Times**, she won the Pulitzer Prize and published two collections, **Living Out Loud** and **Thinking Out Loud**. Her **Newsweek** columns were collected in **Loud and Clear**.

AnnaQuindlen.net
Facebook.com/AnnaQuindlen

# LIKE WHAT YOU'VE READ?

Try these titles by Anna Quindlen,
also available in large print:

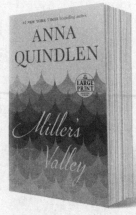

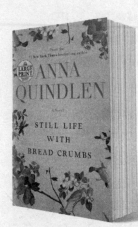

**Miller's Valley**
ISBN 978-0-399-56681-3

**Still Life with
Bread Crumbs**
ISBN 978-0-8041-9439-6

**Alternate Side**
ISBN 978-0-525-63731-8

For more information on large print titles, visit
**www.penguinrandomhouse.com/large-print-format-books**